MANAGING REMOTE STAFF

T0150168

MANAGING REMOTE STAFF
Capitalize on Work-from-Home Productivity

Self-Counsel Press
(a division of)
International Self-Counsel Press Ltd.
Canada USA

Lin Grensing-Pophal

Self-Counsel Press acknowledges the financial support of the Government of Canada through the Canada Book Fund (CBF) for our publishing activities. Canada

Printed in Canada.

First edition: 2020

Library and Archives Canada Cataloguing in Publication

Title: Managing remote staff : capitalize on work-from-home productivity / Lin Grensing-Pophal.

Names: Grensing-Pophal, Lin, 1959- author.

Series: Self-Counsel business series.

Description: Series statement: Business series

Identifiers: Canadiana (print) 2020035664X | Canadiana (ebook) 20200356690 | ISBN 9781770403314 (softcover) | ISBN 9781770405141 (EPUB) | ISBN 9781770405158 (Kindle)

Subjects: LCSH: Supervision of employees. | LCSH: Home-based businesses—Management. | LCSH: Labor productivity.

Classification: LCC HF5549.12 .G74 2020 | DDC 658.3/02—dc23

Self-Counsel Press
(a division of)
International Self-Counsel Press Ltd.

North Vancouver, BC	Bellingham, WA
Canada	USA

CONTENTS

3 BEST JOB TYPES FOR REMOTE WORK 31

4 POLICIES AND PROCEDURES 51

NOTICE TO READERS

Laws are constantly changing. Every effort is made to keep this publication as current as possible. However, the author, the publisher, and the vendor of this book make no representations or warranties regarding the outcome or the use to which the information in this book is put and are not assuming any liability for any claims, losses, or damages arising out of the use of this book. The reader should not rely on the author or the publisher of this book for any professional advice. Please be sure that you have the most recent edition.

INTRODUCTION

On March 13, 2020, President Trump declared a national emergency in the US as those infected with coronavirus around the world neared 100,000. On March 15, the Centers for Disease Control (CDC) recommended gatherings of no more than 50 people in the United States, according to *The New York Times*.

Around this time, in quick succession, a number of heretofore inconceivable events occurred:

- Major League Baseball announced the delay of opening season on March 12; the PGA Tour announced its shutdown the same day.

- Walt Disney World closed on Sunday night, March 15.

- US state/territory stay-at-home orders start on March 15 with Puerto Rico being the first to shut down, followed by California on March 19; by April 3, at least 46 states and Washington, D.C., had ordered nonessential businesses to close.

- By March 17, nearly every state had shut down schools for the remainder of the 2019–2020 school season.

- From childcare centers to institutions of advanced education, students suddenly found themselves working remotely and many parents of K-12 students found themselves stepping into roles as teachers' assistants.

- South by Southwest (SXSW) had taken action even earlier, cancelling its extremely popular and highly attended annual cultural, arts, and music gathering, which was expected to attract more than 400,000 people on March 6.

Suddenly, the world as we knew it had changed dramatically. As businesses of all types and sizes scrambled to serve customers and clients in any way possible, many sent employees home to work.

Even the many stalwart businesses that had long declared that working from home just wasn't an option or couldn't work, found themselves scrambling to find ways to make it work in an environment where the only other alternative was not to operate at all.

It's not an ideal situation, of course, and the virus itself creates or adds to an environment that is not entirely reflective of the positive potential for boosted productivity to the stress and anxiety that is widespread. A Society for Human Management (SHRM) survey exploring the impact of the pandemic on mental health found that 41% of workers said they felt burnout during the pandemic. Nearly one in four, or 23%, felt down, depressed, or hopeless "often." In addition, the research found that certain workers were more at risk of mental health impacts than others — women, younger workers, and those living with a vulnerable person felt these impacts most strongly.

Despite being thrust into a new normal, many businesses and their displaced staff members quickly acclimated to the new normal of remote work. Necessity is, as they say, the mother of invention. It has been fascinating and instructive to watch as various types of organizations have adjusted or totally overhauled their business models to remain viable.

Ashley Sterling, director of operations at The Loop Marketing, in Chicago, says that the biggest adjustment for her has been "the challenge to create a consistent schedule with personal and work life." It's easy, she says, to fall into a "I'll just answer a few emails" rhythm, which can quickly and unexpectedly lead to a work week that spans 50 hours or more. Sterling says that, even after the pandemic, her company will still offer the ability to work remotely and perhaps more than they did before the quarantine. Still, she says, "we all recognize the importance of meeting face-to-face to ensure proper communication."

Two industries that were significantly impacted were education and healthcare. With both K-12 and higher education institutions suddenly closed and having to connect with students, instructors, and parents, the remote instruction options that some had already dabbled with suddenly became mainstream proving that, yes, students can be educated remotely. The situation was similar in healthcare. Telemedicine has been available for some time and many organizations had been offering telehealth services in some form — most notable in behavioral health where demand is high (and getting higher) and providers are in short supply.

The delivery of remote services, of course, requires remote workers. As a long-time advocate of remote work — otherwise known as telecommuting — I've watched with interest as many businesses and business owners who said it couldn't be done have discovered that it could, and must, if they wish to remain viable.

Amid the uncertainty CNBC predicted a number of changes that could become the norm as the country recovers from the coronavirus pandemic. Among them:

- Working in an office could become a status symbol.

- Most meetings could be replaced by email and instant messaging (IM).

- It could be the end of business travel as we know it.

- Office buildings could become "elaborate conference centers."

- Standard "9-to-5" office hours could become a thing of the past.

- Home-office stipends could become a common perk.

Already, many media outlets are predicting that remote work will continue even after the coronavirus abates. A Gartner CFO survey, for instance, indicates that 74% of those surveyed will shift some employees to remote work permanently. By May, 2020, some large tech firms, such as Twitter and Facebook, had already informed their employees that they could "work from home forever."

In May a SmartBrief Workforce reader poll asked this question: "If your employer allowed you to request to work from home (full time or part time), would you?" An astonishing 85% said "yes." When asked if they would be able to continue working from home once their companies reopen, they said:

- Yes, we can continue working remotely full time, if we choose (34.86%).

- Yes, but with limits (32.37%).

- No, the nature of my work requires me to be on site (14.52%).

- No, my employer feels people work better when they're in an office (18.25%).

It's a new normal with businesses, employers, managers, and employees finding that not only is remote work possible, in many, but not all cases, it's preferable.

In the following chapters we'll explore the history of remote work, previously and commonly referred to as telecommuting, and its pros, cons, possibilities, and potential pitfalls. I will offer advice and best practice examples on how to capitalize on the benefits and minimize the potential drawbacks of managing a remote workforce.

Chapter 1

A BRIEF HISTORY OF REMOTE WORK

Even before COVID-19, in the work environment of the twenty-first century, work is being defined differently than it has ever been defined in the past. The "typical" 9:00 a.m. to 5:00 p.m., Monday-to-Friday work week is a thing of the past. Instead, as jobs have become less structured, work has become less structured in terms of how, when, and where it gets done.

In a global, 24/7 world, the notion that all employees of an organization can work the same rigid schedule is obviously far outdated. Punching a time clock is, in fact, an artifact of the industrial revolution and no longer pertinent for what has largely become a service economy. In addition, today's workers value flexibility more than ever, requiring employers that wish to attract and retain the best and the brightest to come up with flexible solutions to meet their needs.

As long ago as the nineteenth century, people were telecommuting. While the term wasn't coined until almost 100 years later, the first person on record who performed work that had previously been done at one business location at a remote location was a

Boston bank president who had a phone line strung from his office to his home in 1877!

1. From the Nineteenth Century to Today

Even as early as the 1950s, location was becoming less and less important to the concept of work. Telephone communications were widely established. And as the make-up of work changed to a more information-based economy following World War II, staff could work more independently, without need of constant supervision.

You've heard of the internet, haven't you? Well, in 1963, a programmer working on the Arpanet Project (the forerunner to today's internet) withdrew from the project to stay home with his wife, who was going through a difficult pregnancy. Another programmer suggested he install an additional phone line in his home so he could program from there. The practice of working from home still didn't have a name, but people were starting to experiment with it.

In 1973, Jack Nilles, a scientist working on NASA satellite communications projects in Los Angeles, coined the term for telecommuting. Now, Nilles is internationally known as the father of telecommuting. He originally used the term to denote "a geographically dispersed office where workers can work at home on a computer and transmit data and documents to a central office via telephone lines." In 1982, Nilles incorporated JALA International, Inc. (www.jala.com). An international group of management consultants, JALA's mission is "to help organizations make effective use of information technology 'telecommunications and computers' and to better cope with the accelerating rate of change in the business environment."

By the time Nilles had come up with a word for the concept of working from locations other than the traditional office, companies were already beginning to experiment with the practice.

In 1978, Blue Cross/Blue Shield of South Carolina had started a cottage-keyer project recognizing that employees could easily perform a number of keyboarding activities at home. In the first year of the project they demonstrated a 26% increase in productivity. In 1980, Mountain Bell started a telecommuting project for its managers. That same year, the US Army launched a telecommuting pilot.

By the mid-1980s, telecommuting was becoming an increasingly popular option. It seemed to address a number of issues, including gridlock, pollution, employee retention, savings on office space, and even increases in productivity.

In 1989, AT&T started a pilot telecommuting program in Los Angeles; the program was expanded to Phoenix in 1990. Employees tried working at home several days per month. AT&T's move in this direction was a voluntary response to Title I of the 1990 Clean Air Act.

In 1992, AT&T introduced a formal telework policy and started its Virtual Workplace training programs. By 1999, more than half of AT&T's managers teleworked at least one day a month; 25% of their managers teleworked one day or more per week and 10% teleworked 100% of the time.

Telecommuting was given a boost in 1990 when amendments to the Clean Air Act mandated employer trip-reduction programs. While telecommuting wasn't a requirement under the Act, it was a recommended way to meet trip-reduction goals and a number of organizations began experimenting with this option. The bill was changed in 1995, and reductions in car-commuter trips are no longer mandatory. However, regional or state rules are still in effect, and telecommuting remains one good way to get cars off the road.

There have been some major changes in telecommuting since its early beginnings. These changes have been driven both by demand and by technology; the internet, email, and cell phones now make it easier than ever to work from virtually any place, at any time.

In the 1990s, there were an estimated 3.7 million workers telecommuting in the United States. In 2000, that number had increased to 6 million. It is also estimated that, by the end of 2009, 14 million people were telecommuting. The rise in these numbers has been driven both by individual and environmental needs.

The entry of Generation Y into the workforce, a demographic that desires flexibility and independence more than those before them, has helped many businesses consider flexible work arrangements as a solution to those desires. Growing concern for the environment has also spurred an increase in telecommuting as a solution for reducing carbon emissions. The increase in technology options that make it easy, if not seamless, for employees to stay connected regardless of physical location has also had a positive impact.

Technology has had a dramatic influence on the workplace and on the ways in which tasks are accomplished. Email, voice mail, and internet technology mean that employees can literally be in touch with their employers 24 hours a day, 7 days a week. The 24/7 culture is changing the way that employees and employers interact; it is changing the very nature of work. Under the old system, employees were tied to the workplace. Tools did not exist to allow contact from remote locations. Today, technology is providing both employers and employees with freedom and flexibility that they would never have imagined even ten short years ago.

Technology is allowing employees to question the status quo and challenge the old ways of doing business. "Why do I need to come to the office to work on a report when I can do it at home on my computer?" "Why can't I access voice mail and email from home?" "Why do I have to be physically located in a phone center to answer customer calls? Why can't I be set up from home to do this?"

And because employers are faced with a shrinking labor market and a growing gap between job seekers' skills and employer needs, more and more are responding to these questions with, "Why not?"

According to Global Workplace Analytics, in 2018, 5 million employees (3.6% of the US workforce) were working at home at least half-time. Working at home has grown 173% since 2005. While the numbers, at least prior to COVID-19 were still relatively low, their research reveals that 56% of employees have jobs that could be done, at least to some degree, remotely.

What does all this mean? It means that businesses must become more flexible and creative in both the recruitment and retention of employees. It means that the traditional brick-and-mortar workplace will soon give way — in fact, has given way, in many places — to a virtual workplace. It means that neither employees nor employers will be hampered by geographic constraints: An employee can live in Florida and work for a company in Georgia, Wisconsin, California, Ontario, Milan, Hong Kong, or literally any of thousands of locations around the globe.

It means that whether they are telecommuting, or simply working in another location as part of a global organization, branch office or "virtual company," the ability to effectively manage off-site staff is no longer a luxury; it has become a necessity for companies that want to compete effectively in this new millennium.

Many already knew this long before 2020 sent shock waves around the globe as companies of all types and in all locations moved quickly to remain open and accessible during the COVID-19 pandemic. That pandemic will likely significantly increase the adoption and widespread acceptance of remote work in a variety of configurations.

Companies large and small, in rural and urban settings, are learning to manage off-site staff relationships effectively. For many, these relationships are simply part of "how we work." For others, they are generated through individual requests. Regardless of the way the need arises, success depends on careful planning and well-established guidelines as well as appropriate selection of both the positions and the people who will work in off-site locations.

Decisions about these arrangements should be made for the right reasons. You should not institute a telecommuting program, for instance, simply because an employee has requested the option or because it seems to be a current trend. Like any other business decision you make, the decision to allow employees to work in nontraditional locations should be based on legitimate and demonstrable business benefits. We explore a number of these in Chapter 2.

2. The Coronavirus Impact on Remote Work

The coronavirus has had a dramatic, immediate, and in most cases unanticipated impact on the work-from-home experience. While the forced experiment has taught some companies and their staff members that remote work has more positive potential than they might have imagined, mandatory work-from-home situations may be negatively impacting productivity according to a study by Digital. com, an independent review website for small business online tools, products, and services, in partnership with YouGov, an authority on public opinion data. Its survey of 2,909 American employees working from home highlighted decreased productivity as a major challenge for employees during the coronavirus.

The key negative impacts identified were lack of prior work-from-home experience and anxiety about the disease. More than half — 54% — of employees said they were working remotely for the first time. Of the 1 in 3 employees who said they had difficulty maintaining efficiency, almost 30% indicated it was primarily due to COVID-19 concerns. Other distractions included having their children or spouse at home with them, and TV or media streaming.

Dealing with the sudden and unexpected need to work from home during a worldwide pandemic is not ideal and, not surprisingly, the experience has taken a toll.

According to research from the Society for Human Resource Management (SHRM) the psychological costs of COVID-19 may be high — 41% of the workers surveyed indicated that they feel burned out; another 23% report feeling depressed. The survey explored the impact of the lockdown on the mental health of US workers. The impacts — negative emotions, concentration issues, and lack of motivation were higher among women, younger workers, and those living with a vulnerable person.

Concerns about the potential impact of the pandemic on their jobs represented a key concern. More than 20% reported that COVID-19 had "threatened the tangible parts of their jobs to a great extent or to a very great extent, including personal opportunities, job security, safe working conditions, and benefits and pay."

But despite the unique pressures felt by employees and their managers during COVID-19, many still feel positive about the long-term potential for working from home as a viable option.

LinkedIn's Workforce Confidence Index poll of 5,447 LinkedIn members from April 27 to May 3, took a look at workers' perspectives on remote work as millions suddenly found themselves displaced to home settings during COVID-19. They asked the question, "Can your industry WFH [work from home] effectively?" By and large respondents answered "yes." This was particularly true in certain industries such as software and IT (82%), finance (82%), and media and communications (76%). Even those in industries that rely heavily on face-to-face contact acknowledged that remote work could have some applications, and we've seen plenty of examples during the coronavirus pandemic — entertainment (44%), recreation and travel (37%), retail (29%).

In June, data released based on a survey commissioned by PGi and conducted by The Harris Poll confirmed that working from home is likely to continue to be a common option in the future. Results indicate that a majority of employed Americans working from home are more productive and are hopeful they will be able to continue to work from home in the future. Video conferencing, respondents said, allows them to collaborate just as well as when participating in face-to-face meetings. Survey respondents included 61% of employed Americans working from home. Of these, 70% say they can get more work done now, primarily because they don't have as many in-person meetings; 63% said they can accomplish more during a video conference meeting than in an in-person meeting; and 41% said working from home has had a very or somewhat positive impact on work/life balance (however, there are mixed results here: 34% said it's had a very or somewhat negative impact). Also, 54% say they would not be comfortable attending large work-related conferences or events.

The coronavirus has provided a forced experiment into how well remote work can serve the needs of businesses of all kinds. For the most part, business owners, managers, and employees have come to believe that remote work can and should be a viable option, now and in the future.

Dawn Michell, VP of human resources at Appian, a low-code automation company based in northern Virginia says: "While I don't want to undermine the stress many of us are under with such limited space between work and personal life, it has caused us to be creative about how we address work and, in some areas, improved it." At Appian, she says, "we've learned how change can prompt creativity and improve areas of our work we didn't expect it to. It's easy for leaders to get stuck in a rut in terms of how they manage and same for employees in terms of how they work."

There will be lessons for employers to learn from the sudden experiment in working from home that the coronavirus prompted.

As leaders, says Andrew Meadows, senior vice president at Ubiquity Retirement + Savings in San Francisco, "we must listen to our employees in terms of what situations provide us with getting the best work from our employees. We don't have to be hovering over them."

Meadows says leaders need to be curious. They need to ask what engages employees; what is the level of engagement; what are the issues; what can be improved; and what can be handled through technology? Maybe, he says, some companies ultimately won't bring their employees back to work physically.

As employers return to whatever awaits them, he cautions employers from being disconnected from whatever the new normal post-pandemic may be. Despite whatever the economy may bring, retention is still extremely important, he says, adding that companies will struggle if they don't listen to their employees.

"Before the COVID-19 pandemic, we were very much an in-office company," says Patricia Elias, chief legal and people officer with ServiceSource. But, she says, "we're proud of how quickly we mobilized our over 3,000 employees worldwide and got everyone set up at home within five days in mid-March, enabling us to keep our employees safe and continue uninterrupted client service." The company has also been pleasantly surprised by the boost in productivity and engagement scores they've seen since moving to a work-from-home model. The company has decided to say with their 100% work-from-home model through at least the end of 2020, she says. "As we look to 2021, we will definitely be expanding our work-from-home model to allow our employees the flexibility that allows them to more seamlessly integrate their work and home lives."

Randstad US, a global staffing company, quickly deployed its 38,000-person global workforce to remote work within just two weeks when the virus hit, says CHRO Jim Link. They've also surveyed employees to see how the shift has been working and, based on the results and on hearing that some employees were ready to get back to the office while others preferred to continue working remotely, have decided to follow a blended and phased approach to reopening, feeling that flexibility is key. They've created three return-to-work models for employees to consider — reopening completely, requiring everyone back onsite, staying fully remote, or a blended approach that has some teams onsite while others work from home.

The ability to work remotely opens up opportunities for employers to staff from a broader pool of candidates, both those who prefer, or must, work from home and those who are located in other geographic settings. Consider, for instance, the challenges that IT companies have long faced in finding technical staff. Removing the local barriers that served to artificially restrict the candidate pool can lead to new opportunities with benefits for both employees and employers.

Even in tight economic times — particularly in tight economic times — business owners want to attract and retain qualified, productive staff members. While rising unemployment rates, fueled by the impacts of the virus, mean that the availability of workers is greater than it was just a few months ago, the availability of highly skilled and highly motivated workers is always at a premium.

And, of course, as the economy improves and aging baby boomers continue to leave the workforce in droves, it will become harder to find talented and qualified employees. The impact on organizations, large and small, will be considerable. Think of your own workforce and the number of employees who will be eligible for retirement in the near future. Think of the key positions that must remain filled with capable and competent staff in order to ensure quality products and services for your customers.

Most employers will agree that the ability to retain employees, regardless of the economy, is always a critical need. To do this, many are looking for creative ways to meet employee needs. Flexibility is one critical area of demand. For many companies, flexibility means providing the opportunity for employees to work remotely.

3. Lessons from the Trenches

Mary Hjorth is executive vice president and CHRO with Kestra Financial, with headquarters in Austin, Texas, and offices in 30 cities. A major lesson that she believes companies have learned during the pandemic: "We can work from home and be productive." At Kestra Financial, she says, "we were more than surprised at how well it worked." Kestra had traditionally maintained a structure of working from the office because of collaboration and its culture for getting work done, she says. But, now, she says, "Working from home can work as well. Our employees are resilient during a crisis."

Although the company operates from 30 locations, she says, "getting aligned was not as difficult as we assumed because our tech team was prepared. Because we're a financial services company, we had to be prepared for any situation. We had a continuity plan and had tested the plan, and our virtual network and our phones."

Now, Hjorth says, the company is crafting policies for long-term working from home situations and for post-COVID. There will be situations in which employees work remotely every day; some will work remotely two or three days a week; some perhaps one day a week. "We need to be thoughtful about space and maintaining space between employees when they are in the office. We also need to build what-if scenarios into our policies."

For instance, she says, "If we find that 25% want to be in the office and 25% want to work from home, we no longer need our current office space, for example. How will we assign space? Will we use hoteling areas for people who need to come in the office periodically? Will we assign flex space?"

Another positive benefit from this experience: "We've learned that a WFH policy will allow us to open the talent pool. We can draw employees from anywhere," she said.

"So far, we've gotten great feedback from our employees, which showed they do care about their jobs and their productivity."

Hjorth also says it's been gratifying to watch leadership in action. "It's amazing to watch our President and CEO James Poer. It was amazing in how he conducted his role and the funds he made available for ensuring we could deploy our employees to work from home when the pandemic hit. He didn't put up barriers.

"Although there were a lot of unknowns, he made wise decisions. Now, he creates a weekly video from his backyard to help maintain our culture."

That's another lesson of the pandemic, Hjorth says. "You learn a lot about your leadership. In a time of crisis, you learn quickly that there can be a new way of doing business. It's gratifying to experience true leadership during a crisis."

Kestra announced recently to employees that certain positions could work from home on a more permanent basis. They're also preparing to move more teams into remote work situations.

"Our focus now is to training our managers on how to manage remotely. The concept of constant communications can't be ignored," Hjorth says. "We have regular check-ins, but they aren't just about productivity. They need to cover wellness, safety, how to manage home life while working."

A pulse survey shows that employees are happy with the way the company has handled the transition to remote teams. Still, opinions are split into two camps: those who love it and those who prefer to work in the office. A full survey will be conducted as usual later in the year of the firm's 550 employees.

Hjorth's advice to other employers considering a long-term move to WFH:

- Take a survey to ensure you understand your employees' needs.

- Understand what your leaders expect from remote employees.

- Make sure it's not an HR-driven policy.

- Assess the types of employees who are going to be most successful working from home. It's likely that nearly every group could work from home. For example, perhaps your mail room and cashier groups need to work from the office. Do others?

- Assess any legal ramifications such as data security, employee privacy and productivity.

- Add policies to your employee handbook. Consider how to approach whether employees will need to sign a document acknowledging WFH policies.

"We have witnessed change for our employees," she said. "They have proven to us that we were wrong to assume they needed to be in the office. It's a new world."

Chapter 2

MYTHS, MISCONCEPTIONS, PROS, AND CONS

The prospect of managing employees remotely continues to unnerve, even scare, many managers. The idea of being responsible for the work of people who are off-site can be threatening, yet is also often entirely misunderstood. Consider, for example, the banking industry, which has multiple branch locations where employees may physically be located, yet they work for managers who may be located in the corporate office. Or multinational, global firms with employees who may be dispersed in work settings around the globe. In both of these scenarios, employees may rarely work face-to-face with their managers and other colleagues — yet they must still work with these other staff members to get their work done.

The same is true in any remote work environment.

The point here is that managing remote workers should not be a concept that is feared or one that is entirely unknown. In fact, as many companies have learned during the pandemic, remote work is an option available to companies today that can add flexibility and value for both employees and managers.

Still, a number of myths and misconceptions prevail.

1. Exploring Some Myths about Remote Work

Jessica Lambrecht with The Rise Journey has worked with small businesses for more than 15 years, "primarily long-standing organizations that were well-established before remote work was truly a functional possibility," she says. In her work, though, she's found that "most of these predominantly in-person organizations have almost effortlessly embraced a virtual workplace, with overall positive results." Two of the main misconceptions that present challenges, she says, are that people think —

- setting up remote capabilities is too complicated, and

- employees won't be as productive if they're not in the office.

Neither, she says, is true. "As for productivity, it's often a bias many owners and managers hold due to a lack of remote experience," she says. "With time savings in commuting, in-person inefficiencies — like water coolers — and a focus-savings via a reduction in stress from traffic, childcare responsibilities, and more, employees often find their productivity increases greatly when working from home."

Like many myths and misconceptions, the reasons some myths may prevail is because there is some truth to them. However, just because certain misconceptions may be provable, doesn't mean they have to persist, or that there are not opportunities to minimize or entirely eliminate whatever issues are driving these myths. Here we explore some of the more common myths.

1.1 Myth 1: Employees will be too isolated and will become alienated from the team

The fear of isolation is an issue for employees; it is also a concern for employers. Isolation may be a misconception, however. Gallup, for instance, has found that while remote workers certainly can suffer from feelings of loneliness and isolation, this isn't typical and is preventable. Gallup points to a Buffer study of 1,900 remote workers globally which found that "90% intend to work remotely for the rest of their lives and 94% recommend off-site careers." Only 21% indicated that "loneliness" was their biggest struggle while working remotely.

While there is certainly potential for isolation when employees are working from remote locations and are not physically located near coworkers, isolation is not a certainty. Much can be done to ensure that there is regular and meaningful contact between the telecommuter and other team members. We'll explore these opportunities in Chapters 9 and 10.

1.2 Myth 2: If an employee wants to work remotely, they'll be out of the office five days a week

Remote work isn't necessarily an all-or-nothing proposition. While some employees do literally work in a remote location eight hours a day, five days a week, arrangements are varied and dependent on the employees' and the employers' unique needs. According to Global Workplace Analytics, "two to three days a week seems to be the sweet spot that allows for a balance of concentrative work (and home) and collaborative work (at the office)."

A key point here is that remote work does not have a single definition. There are a wide range of variations and options driven not only by the type of work being done, but by employee and management preferences and workplace cultures. In fact, while we often refer to employees working in non-work locations as "working from home," they could be working from a coffee shop, a park, a beach, or virtually (pun intended) anywhere.

1.3 Myth 3: If I let one employee telecommute, I'll have to let all employees have the opportunity

Not every job is appropriate for telecommuting and neither is every employee. Many manufacturing jobs, for instance, must be done on site. Similarly, some employees may require direct supervision or may not have demonstrated a high enough level of competency to make them good candidates for a work-from-home arrangement. We'll explore the characteristics of traits that effective remote workers share in Chapter 6.

The bottom line is that the decision must be made collectively by the company, the manager, and the employee involved. Having the option for remote work does not guarantee that every employee will be able to take advantage of that option automatically. Part of the process involves establishing clear guidelines, standards, and policies, which we'll cover in Chapters 4, 9, and 11.

1.4 Myth 4: Everyone will want to work remotely and there will be nobody left in the office

Just as you may not want certain employees to work from home, you may have employees who prefer the standard workplace environment, as Hjorth's employee sentiments support. Many employees enjoy the social aspects of work. They like the interactions with others, and the opportunity to leave home and enter a different environment. For those people, working remotely is unlikely to become a preferred option. As a manager, you are in control of how you staff your department. There are some managers of workforces comprised entirely of remote workers where the manager may be working remotely too. There are others who, for whatever reasons, do not find that remote work is a viable option. And there are many, many more who find that the right solution is somewhere in between. Ultimately, though, you are responsible for staffing your workforce to provide optimum service to your internal and external customers.

1.5 Myth 5: Only big companies are involved in telecommuting

This is certainly not true. While there are many very large firms that embraced WFH long before COVID-19 emerged (in fact, according to FlexJobs' list of "20 Companies That Consistently Have the Remote Jobs," companies on the list include Kelly Services, UnitedHealth Group, Anthem, Inc., ADP, Humana, Salesforce, and Pearson, among others), the ability to do remote work exists in companies that run the gamut from small firms with only a handful of employees to multinational firms.

1.6 Myth 6: It is too difficult to manage remote workers

As we'll see, in many ways managing remote workers is really no different than effectively managing employees in any type of role. Remote workers and the companies they work for consistently say that good managers are good managers, regardless of whether they're managing someone in the office or from a remote location. The skills are the same, as we'll see in Chapter 9.

There are a number of benefits of working remotely, for both companies/employers and employees. There are drawbacks as well. It's important to explore and understand both.

2. Benefits of Remote Work for Companies/Employers

Despite an economy that has rapidly shifted from one where employers were struggling to attract and retain top talent to one where unemployment levels are reaching those seen during the Great Depression, providing flexible options for employees remains important for a number of reasons, not the least of which is the impact on morale and engagement.

Today's employees crave flexibility and the positive impact on work/life balance that it can bring. According to research from FlexJobs, "16 percent of the 7,300 workers who responded to its annual survey said they are currently searching for a new job because of flexibility issues. Eight percent (up from 75 percent in 2018) said that they would be more loyal to their employers if they had flexible work options." It's interesting to note that 52% of those responding indicated that they had tried to negotiate flexible work arrangements with their employers. In addition, more than 25% said they would trade pay — as much as a 10–20% cut — for more flexibility.

There are bottom line benefits as well. According to data collected by Atlas VPN, US companies could save as much as $4.5 trillion a year by 2030. Much of this is related to a boost in productivity; 37% of companies said that allowing staff to work from home increased productivity by about 40%.

In addition, depending on the company and the way it has structured its remote work options and the balance between on and offsite staff, there may be significant real estate savings.

According to Global Workplace Analytics, the average real estate savings for companies with full-time teleworkers is $10,000/ employee/year.

Employers are often initially hesitant to allow employees to work from home, primarily due to concerns that lack of physical presence will lead to lack of involvement on the part of the employee. However, as this data and other studies indicate, those that have allowed employees to work from home have been surprised to find that productivity actually increases, and employees report higher job satisfaction and improved morale. Alongside reduced real estate costs, many companies have also found that their absenteeism and turnover rates have declined after instituting work-from-home programs.

Another big benefit is access to a broader talent pool.

The labor pool has experienced some significant fluctuations over the past few years. It is sometimes difficult to find skilled, qualified, and motivated employees. Telecommuting (and the technology that goes with it) makes it possible to bypass the boundaries of geography. For employers, that means the ability to select from a much broader pool of talent. It also means that barriers are removed when, for instance, a merger moves the corporate headquarters to a new location and a number of highly skilled employees, unable or unwilling to relocate, now have the option of continuing to work for the company, but from their homes.

Here are some additional benefits of remote work that employers point to:

- **Reduced sick time:** Employers find that telecommuters have fewer sick days — an average of one to two days a year. It makes sense. There are times when a cold may make the thought of spending the day at the office seem like torture, but you might be perfectly able to function.

- **Positive environmental impact:** While the US Clean Air Act was changed in 1995 and no longer makes reductions in car-commuter trips mandatory, and further environmental laws may be forthcoming, environmentally aware employers know that telecommuting can have a positive impact on traffic congestion and, ultimately, emissions. In fact, during the COVID-19 pandemic there were reports globally about the positive impact on the environment presumably due to fewer cars on the road.

- **Reduction in traffic:** In Atlanta, companies began implementing telecommuting during the summer Olympics of 1996 when traffic, related not only to the event but also to event preparation, created difficulties for commuters. That experience drove early interest in telecommuting, but the impacts of heavy traffic are still being felt around the globe — working from home is an opportunity for positive impact.

- **Safety issues related to weather conditions:** In northern climates, telecommuting means that snow days are a thing of the past. When you have only to commute on foot from one room to another in your house, bad weather is no longer a barrier.

- **Enhanced opportunities for disabled individuals:** Telecommuting provides a workable and effective way to accommodate employees with various health problems and disabilities that might otherwise keep them out of the labor market. Far beyond complying with legal regulations, the option of working from home can allow employers to provide highly qualified but disabled employees with the opportunity to contribute their talents toward meaningful endeavors.

- **Impact on employer brand — improved attractiveness of company to job candidates:** Employees are, more than ever, giving their personal lives precedence over their professional lives. To many, the ability to work in a flexible environment is very attractive. Even those employees who are not interested in telecommuting may perceive a company that offers the option as being progressive and concerned with meeting the needs of its employees.

One of the most significant of these benefits, perhaps, is access to a broader labor pool. As Andrew Meadows, senior vice president at Ubiquity Retirement + Savings in San Francisco, a company that employs 85 staff members — 85% working from home — says: "The best talent isn't necessarily within 50 miles of your organization. The best talent can be anywhere. It can be the key to innovation."

Remote work isn't without some potential drawbacks, however, and it's important to explore these as well.

3. Drawbacks of Remote Work for Companies/Employers

There is good reason that some employers and their managers/ supervisors balk at the idea of allowing employees to work remotely. There are some legitimate drawbacks. These include:

- **Resistance to change among both employees and managers:** The popularity of remote work or work-from-home options has been driven largely by employees who, because of their unique personal needs, have requested flexible options for accomplishing their duties. While some employers were early adopters of telecommuting as a work option decades ago, and while studies continue to show that more and more companies are offering employees the opportunity to work remotely, many have been resistant to change. Some employers see no need to change a system that has worked for decades and, as most of us can relate to, change can be personally and organizationally challenging. Employers who decide to explore work-from-home options should not be surprised to experience some resistance from both managers and employees, even after the COVID-19 experience. In fact, negative experiences with working from home during the pandemic may serve to fuel this resistance.

- **The belief that "out of sight" will mean "out of mind":** Front-line managers have tended to be the most resistant to supervising workers who are in other locations. They believe that employees who are not physically present will be impossible to oversee. "How can I tell whether they're really working?," they ask. "I'm just not comfortable with the idea of letting employees work from home," others say. This can be a relatively easy objection to dispel, though. Consider how often managers actually oversee the work of their employees in a traditional setting. Managers may be physically located in an area removed from their staff. They may be involved in numerous meetings and other activities throughout the day that preclude direct observation of employees. And, of course, they have their own work to do, meaning that it is very unlikely that they are actually observing employees in the workplace to any great degree.

- **Potential for abuse of the option:** Are there employees who will take advantage of the opportunity to work from home? Employees who may look at this flexible option as a way of saving money on childcare costs while allowing them plenty of time for interaction with the kids? Employees who will spend their time engaged in personal activities instead of concentrating on their assigned work responsibilities? Certainly. But these individuals would be unproductive in any type of setting. A good selection process will serve to screen out these individuals before they are able to take part in a work-from-home program. In addition, careful development of specific and measurable goals and objectives can provide management with an objective method of monitoring performance.

- **Offering remote work options will require greater coordination:** Companies may be hesitant to allow remote work options because they fear that it will demand greater coordination and require more time and effort than the management of traditional staff. This may be true initially as the program is being developed and as the organization is adapting to it. In the long run, however, managing remote workers can strengthen all management practices by helping the organization focus more on outcome than process in the management of staff activities.

- **Remote work may have a negative impact on communication:** Communication is certainly a challenge when employees are no longer physically located with the majority of their workgroup and when you can't simply walk down the hall to interact. Communication is a challenge in any work setting, however, and as with the coordination of work activities, the communication needs driven by remote work may actually serve to improve communication overall within the organization. Special communication challenges are not unique to telecommuting. Many companies operate globally today, with employees spread around the world. Fortunately, the technology that is now readily available to virtually anyone (at a very reasonable cost) means that distance is no longer relevant.

- **Legal and accounting issues:** All employers have legal rights and responsibilities with respect to their employees; remote-work options simply create different issues. For example, one of the largest areas of concern is for the safety of employees in a home office, or workers' compensation. Another concern that may develop is the one of wage and hour laws (i.e., when will the telecommuter be eligible for overtime pay?). We'll explore these issues in more detail in Chapter 4.

Conflict between on- and off-site workers: Remote work is not appropriate for all people. Your decision on whether or not to allow an employee to work from home is likely to be based both on the requirements of the job and the individual characteristics of the employee. Working from home or from some other remote location is an attractive option, and it is not unlikely that the employees who are unable to take advantage of it will feel some resentment toward those who are. Conflict may escalate if communication or hand-offs become problematic.

- **Initial cost of setup:** Some people may be opposed to telecommuting because of concern over the costs involved. Costs will, of course, vary depending on the job that needs to be done, but generally speaking, it should cost no more to set up an employee to work from home than it does to accommodate the employee at the normal work setting. In fact, many companies have documented substantial savings in office space and equipment needs. Careful planning is the key to controlling costs, as is common sense. A telecommuter may have the need to make photocopies from time to time, but that does not necessarily mean that he or she should be provided with a photocopier for his or her home office.

- **Negative impact on teamwork:** There is something to be said about the camaraderie that develops between a group of people working together, day after day, within the same work environment. And it can certainly be challenging for a manager to build and maintain that same sense of team when some of the team members are seemingly absent. But it can be done.

Still, the option, especially given the impact of the pandemic, is one that is likely to cause even the greatest resisters to reconsider offering a remote option. One compelling reason: It can have a big impact on employee retention.

As Zenefits reports, based on a survey of employees, 36% indicated that they strongly or somewhat agreed that they were likely to leave their current employer in the next 12 months because it didn't offer flexible arrangements. While 28% strongly disagreed, the numbers are compelling enough to give employers pause when considering offering flexibility. In addition, 44% said they strongly agreed (33% somewhat agreed) that flexible work arrangements would be an important factor when evaluating future job opportunities.

Employees see some significant benefits in the option. One factor that many employees indicated that they strongly agreed with, and which also provide benefit to employers is that "flexible work arrangements would or do allow me to be more productive" — 47% strong agreed with that statement; 31% somewhat agreed.

4. Benefits of Remote Work for Employees

Employees enjoy the flexibility of telecommuting as well as reduced commuting expenses and hassles. They are better able to balance the demands of home and work; they report reduced stress and higher productivity, and demonstrate a strong sense of loyalty and commitment to those organizations that recognize and respond to their personal needs.

They enjoy:

- **Reduced or eliminated commute time:** In major metropolitan areas and even in some smaller communities, a daily commute may mean putting up with traffic, congestion, long wait times, and frustration. Telecommuting eliminates these concerns — and allows employees to save money on gasoline, vehicle maintenance, and other travel-related costs. The elimination of a one-hour, round-trip commute each day results in a savings of six full weeks of work per year.

- **Flexibility:** Formerly, employees were confined to their work areas from a certain time in the morning until a certain time in the afternoon, for a specific number of days each week. They were generally allowed one break in the morning and one in the afternoon (both at predetermined times) and a lunch period of anywhere from 15 minutes to an hour. To put it simply, their time was rigidly controlled and governed by the needs (or, more precisely, the whims) of their employers.

  As employees have become more independent and the employment options available to them have increased, they have begun to question this rigidity and to request — even demand — flexibility in how their time is scheduled. Telecommuting responds to these requests by recognizing that it is no longer a "9-to-5" world. Today's employees, if provided with the appropriate work tools and communication channels, can effectively work any time during the 24-hour day — seven days a week.

- **An environment free of disruptions:** The workplace can be very distracting and may result in lost productivity. Telecommuters frequently report (and companies agree) that employees are more productive because they have greater privacy and fewer unplanned interruptions of their time. COVID-19 has changed this, of course, with many employees sharing their work-at-home space with spouses and partners, caring for and teaching children whose schools have closed, and in some cases also caring for parents or other adults. Still, even many of those working from home during the pandemic are reporting greater productivity, according to research by Prodoscore, an employee productivity tool. Through an evaluation of 100 million data points across 30,000 users, Prodoscore determined that remote workers had been 47% more productive in March and April 2020, during the pandemic while working from home. Specifically, they found the following happened:

- The average worker starts work at 8:32 a.m. and stops at 5:38 p.m.

- Tuesday, Wednesday, and Thursday are the most productive days, in that order.

- The most productive period during the day is from 10:30 a.m. to 3:00 p.m.

- Employee "ramp-up" to being productive takes one to three hours daily.

Contrary to concerns that managers have long had about the impact of working from home on productivity, Prodoscore data and other research continues to suggest that the opposite is true:

- **Ability to balance work and home demands:** Employees who are able to work from home often are better able to balance the demands of work with the demands and personal needs of their home lives. Raising young children, caring for older parents, pursuing hobbies and personal interests; all this can be accomplished with less stress and frustration when the traditional concept of work is changed to one that recognizes the needs of the employee.

- **Decrease in miscellaneous expenses (e.g., clothing, meals):** As any employee knows, there are a lot of miscellaneous expenses associated with working, including transportation costs, clothing, and food. Telecommuters are able to save on these costs, which results in a positive impact on their disposable income.

- **Elimination of transportation problems:** Telecommuting eliminates travel concerns for employees in areas where winter can mean snowy and icy roads — and days when they simply can't safely get to work.

According to a study by atlasvpn:

- 65% of employees are more productive working from home

- 80% of employees concentrate better without their colleagues around

- 77% of employees find more time to be productive outside 9 to 5 hours

- 85% of businesses agree that location flexibility can increase productivity

- 37% of companies confirmed that letting staff work remotely increased productivity by 40%

Working from home, though, doesn't appeal to everyone and there are some drawbacks that both employers and employees should be aware of.

5. Drawbacks of Remote Work for Employees

Not all employees are anxious to work from home. In fact, employees harbor a number of fears about leaving the relative comfort and security of a traditional workplace. As a manager it is important that you understand some of these concerns and that you're able to directly and candidly discuss them with staff members. There are disadvantages to telecommuting and, for some employees, these disadvantages can be insurmountable. These can include:

- **Isolation:** One of the real benefits of working at the office is the social interaction with other people. While people working remotely still have ample opportunity for communication with those still located on site — through email, phone, video conference, and in-person meetings — the fact remains that a lot of time will be spent alone. While some employees may thrive in this type of environment, others may find the isolation difficult to deal with.

- **Home distractions:** People working from their homes often have difficulty creating an appropriate boundary between home and work. Friends, family, and neighbors may perceive that the at-home employee is more receptive to drop-in visits, phone calls, and other interruptions.

  People working from home whose arrangements allow them to work with their children present have other distractions. That has certainly been the experience for many of those who were sent home to work during the pandemic. And, of course, there are the distractions that people working from home create for themselves: the temptations of nice, sunny days; the lure of the television; the unrelenting desire to throw in a load of laundry.

- **Workaholism:** The difficulty of drawing a distinction between home and work may create a problem of overdedication to the job. Employees working off-site are often tempted to work longer hours and can find it difficult to create appropriate boundaries between work responsibilities and personal needs. When the office is always just steps away, the lure of completing a project, checking email, or doing just one more thing can be strong.

- **Limited access to computers, copy machines, and other office resources and services:** While you will want to consider carefully each employee's needs in terms of work equipment and tools, depending on the employee and his or her job, you may not be able to justify providing every piece of office equipment available for the home office. An employee may need to rely on administrative assistance at the head office or plan occasional trips into the office to take care of routine tasks.

- **Invisibility — a career killer:** Employees may be hesitant to pursue work-at-home options because they have come to view it as a career killer. They fear that if they aren't continually involved, they will be overlooked for key projects, assignments, and promotions. This is a very real concern. However, a study by the Lally School of Management at Rensselaer Polytechnic Institute found that this concern may be overblown. Using a sample of more than 400 employees matched with promotion and salary data, researcher and professor Timothy D. Golden found that whether telecommuting had a negative impact on an employee's work depended on "the employee's work context." Those in companies where telecommuting was largely accepted and practiced were promoted more, for instance, than those in settings where telecommuting was relatively rare. In addition, his analysis suggested that those who worked more than required of them "benefited in terms of both promotions and salary growth." ("Telecommuting found to have little impact on corporate careers," ScienceDaily.com, accessed August, 2020).

Typically, it is the most independent and self-motivated individuals who are good candidates for telecommuting — the same traits that characterize upwardly mobile employees in general. As a manager, one of your key responsibilities is employee development. Employees working off-site, as part of the staff, need to be part of this process.

Remote work is on the rise, spurred in 2020 by the sudden need to work remotely because of the pandemic but, regardless of what has prompted a resurgence in considering this flexible option, remote work is likely here to stay.

Littler, a labor and employment firm with more than 1,500 attorneys in offices around the world, has conducted research on companies' return-to-work plans related to the pandemic. The COVID-19 Return to Work Survey Report, completed by 1010 in-house counsel, HR professionals, and C-suite executives, revealed that half of all respondents were not only considering the option of continuing to allow employees to work from home, but where considering requiring more employees to work from home (with 20% indicating that they have done this "to a great extent" and 30% saying that they have done this "somewhat" — in an effort to reduce physical office costs, including real estate). After reopening, 52% indicate they are likely to be more flexible in accommodating valid requests to work remotely; 30% say they plan to change their remote work policies to increasingly allow employees to work remotely.

6. Lessons from the Trenches

As a CMO that works remotely, who has hired others to work remotely, and who has onboarded new staff remotely, Morgan Taylor, CMO for LetMeBank, has had a crash course in managing off-site employees during the pandemic, but was fortunate to have had some prior experience working from home.

"We started working from home before the current crisis began, and while we weren't sure how this would work out, on paper it sounded like a good idea," he says. "You quickly realize it has some challenges. Getting used to working in the place you traditionally rest is something that takes some getting used to, for example. Home broadband speeds need to be good enough, and you need emergency ways to get in contact if things go down."

Still, he says, the benefits far outweigh the downsides and he predicts that "a lot of companies will be realizing that."

Why spend money on a big shared workspace when everyone has proven they can do the same work from home, and are happier doing so? Currently they are all itching to leave the house as they've been told not to, but not specifically for the office. Under normal circumstances, the idea of working from home quickly becomes very appealing to employers and employees.

Before working from home, says Taylor, it was possible to easily spend four hours a day going to and from work. "Once you realize this is all wasted time, giving up those four hours again seems like torture."

Happier team members, he says, are more efficient team members. "After the initial battle to set up a home workspace has been concluded, everyone starts to realize it's more efficient when possible to use remote workers."

It's a misconception, Taylor says, "that remote workers, away from the watchful eye of their boss, will start watching Netflix and doing no work. It's a hard preconception to shake, even though it's totally wrong." The virus, he says, has forced employers into a situation where they've been able to see, firsthand, that team members can be efficient while working remotely.

To a large degree, while the virus really forced employers' hands in terms of trying a work-from-home model, technology has proven to be an aid for allowing the kind of communication and interactions required — between employees and colleagues as well as between employees and customers and others — that now make it possible for a wide range of jobs to be performed remotely.

Chapter 3

BEST JOB TYPES FOR REMOTE WORK

There are certain types of jobs that have involved working from re-mote or off-site locations for years. Salespeople, for instance, have traditionally operated out of places other than a typical office set-ting. They may work on the road or they may work from their homes.

Freelance writers for major magazines work from their homes or from remote locations, and are often not physically located in the office, or even in the city, where the magazine is located.

Telemarketers and call center staff members often do not require a centralized location, but may operate virtually from their homes or satellite centers. As long as they have the communication equipment and computer information they need to sell the company's products and services, where they sell those products and respond to custom-er questions really doesn't make a difference.

And, of course, the computer industry and digital marketing are areas where remote work is common.

Even though employers broadly learned that many jobs they thought could not be done remotely could during the pandemic, there are still some jobs that simply need to be performed in a work setting. Some obvious examples are restaurant servers, checkout clerks in grocery stores or retail settings, childcare workers, and many workers in manufacturing settings.

But, with the rapid changes being made in technology and in the way we view work, and with some creative solutions, even some of these jobs may eventually be appropriate for off-site work. For instance, not that long ago, most people would have said that healthcare providers could not be located outside of traditional healthcare settings that, of course, they needed to be able to interact face-to-face with their patients. That is, of course, no longer the case.

As telehealth has expanded, and has been fueled by the pandemic through the loosening up of restrictions and easing of barriers to reimbursement for providers, it's clear that certain types of care can be provided remotely. In fact, in some areas there are big benefits to doing so. Behavioral health is one notable example. It's an area where a severe shortage of providers negatively impacts many people who need care but don't have access where they live; this is true, especially, in rural settings. Telehealth, though, allows these patients to connect with providers and receive care no matter where they are. In fact, experts predict that the coronavirus care experience will serve to rapidly expand and extend telehealth as an option. In the article "Telehealth set for 'tsunami of growth,' says Frost & Sullivan," (Healthcare ITNews, accessed August, 2020), the study "Telehealth: A Technology-Based Weapon in the War Against the Coronavirus," was discussed and it said "researchers predict that the pandemic will continue to reshape care delivery and open big opportunities for virtual care in the near-term future." They also point out that Frost & Sullivan has forecast a sevenfold growth in telehealth by 2025.

Educational institutions also were hard hit by the pandemic, sending students and teachers home in spring 2020. According to Education Week: "At their peak, the closures affected at least 55.1 million students in 1,234,000 US public and private schools." While higher education institutions and private industry organizations such as Coursera and Khan Academy had already been doing distant learning for some time, the rapid expansion caused by the shutdowns during the pandemic raise the prospect of enhanced opportunities for the future, at all levels of education.

Some jobs, of course, lend themselves more readily to the prospect of working from home. The Balance Careers published a list of these in 2020 called "The Best Jobs to Work Remotely" (accessed August, 2020).

They include:

- Customer service

- Entry-level computer jobs

- Computer programming

- Sales

- Teachers and tutors

- Data entry, coding, and transcription

- Translation

- Medical billing and coding

- Web developer, and graphic designer

- Freelance writing

- Teaching English as a second language (TESL/TEFL)

- Android or iOS developing

Others are highly unlikely to ever be possible to do from a remote location — childcare workers, for instance. Manufacturing is another area where, on the surface, it would seem that jobs must be performed onsite as workers use machinery to produce products of various types. It's an industry that was particularly challenged during the pandemic — unable to produce various goods without employees onsite and criticized in some cases for not sending workers home. Employees in warehouse settings also must work on site; a dangerous prospect during the pandemic. Amazon has come under widespread criticism from employees and others for the pressure employees faced during the pandemic and their potential exposure to the disease. Warehouse workers have to be onsite to move and load products; truckers and delivery service workers, in turn, must be on the job physically.

Yet, who knows? Technology is evolving to allow us to do amazing things that we might not have even imagined just a few short years ago.

1. Is Your Business Ready to Manage Off-site Staff?

At the end of 2019, if asked this question, many businesses and managers would likely have said "no." By mid-2020, though, many of those sample people having experienced first-hand that it could be done would likely offer a "maybe."

There have been many lessons learned during the COVID-19 pandemic about what works, what doesn't, and what might work better in the future in terms of working with off-site staff.

1.1 Lessons from the pandemic

Remote work reached a tipping point in 2020. According to a survey from biz-tech consultancy West Monroe, the top priority for more than one-third of C-suite executives during the coronavirus pandemic was managing a remote workforce scoring higher, even, than cutting expenses. Forty two percent of the respondents said that the crisis would fundamentally alter their organization's approach to remote working in the long term.

Jessica Lambrecht, founder of The Rise Journey, has worked with businesses for more than 15 years, primarily longstanding organizations that were well-established before remote work became possible. Most, she says, have come to "almost effortlessly embrace a virtual workplace with overall positive results." One organization, she says, "was able to organize a ten-person team with no remote work history into a virtual workspace overnight." They scheduled daily conference calls to discuss priorities and a shared Google doc to coordinate workflow. That's it!

Kelly Palmer, CLO at Degreed, an education technology company, says: "The workforce will not return to normal after the pandemic. Workers have experienced a taste of what agility and autonomous working feels like — working on their own terms, at a place of their choosing, on projects aligned with their skills and interests. HR must recognize that a shift in workplace dynamics has occurred, now people are going to ask for more flexibility and autonomy to do work that interests them and builds their skills. By recognizing and feeding this desire, organizations can stand out in the future as an employer of choice, attracting the best talent and turning the workforce into a competitive differentiator."

Dana Case is director of operations at MyCorporation.com. She says: "COVID-19 was an unprecedented event and even more unprecedented in uprooting so many working professionals into a radically different type of remote work environment — only working from home due to safety/shelter in place rules. I think the biggest misconception being challenged is that a remote worker is out of contact. Remote workers are working and sticking to their traditional workplace schedules, not watching Netflix all day. Our team has been extremely active and 'on' while working remote, able to reach through a quick Zoom call, email, text, or Slack message— or all of the above."

Filip Silobod is the owner of Honest Marketing, a digital marketing agency in Ireland. He says: "I think the COVID-19 situation will have a big impact on remote working globally. Employers who were against remote are forced to let workers work remotely/from home. The mass remote work forces companies to create rules, guides and to test what works for them while working remotely. Once they find a system that works, e.g., like a timetable or workflow for a remote worker that works best for them, they will be more open to hiring a remote worker because they can put them in that system. The barrier will be removed if remote is successful for them in this period.

"For a lot of workers who wanted to work from home, this is their chance to finally do so full time. Those who like it will want to continue working from home. So that will put pressure on employers to continue giving remote work. I'm sure many will feel that the optimal way is a mix of remote and office work so I expect there will be much more workers working part remote, part in the office."

Cecile Alper-Leroux, is VP, HCM innovation at Ultimate Software. She says: "While many tech companies have had remote work-friendly policies in place for years, this pandemic has forced many more traditional face-time industries to experiment with distributed work. This opens the conversation to creating more choice and voice for employees. We now know for sure that remote work is operationally possible for many more employees than organizations ever believed possible before the current health crisis. When offices eventually reopen, it's likely that some people who had to work remotely for the first time, and enjoyed it, will advocate for the ability to do so permanently or at least intermittently. Organizations will have to be more open to nontraditional work arrangements after investing in collaboration solutions and remote systems that had to be put in place for business continuity — and what's more, businesses may see unexpected cost savings that will make them rethink additional office space investments — this is of course only if the remote work experiment yields positive business results.

"This change to more remote work could be particularly welcome for employees with both visible and invisible disabilities — as some disabled employees have faced significant barriers to work and workplaces due to inflexible or nonexistent investment in work adaptations. With more people working remotely as a result of the coronavirus, people who have never experienced such barriers now understand what it means to need an adjustment at work, whether that means flexible hours to manage childcare, needing closed captioning for meetings due to disruptive background noise, or specialized equipment to make working from home more comfortable and sustainable. My hope is that more people will bring a deeper understanding and an element of empathy into the workplace once the crisis has passed."

Although more companies than might have previously believed it to be the case have found themselves able to manage employees remotely, not all would agree that this is the ideal situation. Others have discovered, firsthand, process improvements required to make remote management more successful.

1.2 What it takes: Traits of companies most effective in managing remote staff

Some of the key traits required of companies hoping to effectively and productively manage off-site staff include:

- **Commitment and support from management:** If yours is a small, independently owned business managed primarily by you, you can move forward with various flexible work options with few problems. The larger your business and the more management staff involved, however, the more work that needs to be done to encourage commitment and support from management. Managing remote workers will not be as effective if policies, practices, and processes are applied inconsistently throughout the organization. For example, if one manager permits an employee to work from home one day a week, but another refuses to consider the option.

- **Selection at the department level:** Individual managers and supervisors need to be responsible for selecting the positions and individuals that should or could be located off-site. This is part of managing a department. While the rules and criteria should be applied consistently from an overall business standpoint, it is important that actual selection of positions which are appropriate for remote work and individuals who have the traits to work remotely effectively occurs with input at the department level.

- **Support through equipment and access to other key resources:** Employees can't just be sent home and told to "make it work." They need tools and access to resources just as employees on-site do. This may include computer equipment, telephone and other devices, as well as access to information, training, and other materials that can usually be readily accessed remotely.

- **Clear guidelines:** Clear guidelines are key, particularly when decisions are being made more for personal preference than business necessity. Guidelines should be carefully considered, thoroughly documented and communicated, and consistently applied. The guidelines should indicate to employees and managers what criteria are needed for approving off-site work arrangements, how employees might request consideration for these opportunities, and what the requirements are for ongoing participation. Consistency in the application of these guidelines is important.

- **A contract/agreement outlining the variance in work relationship:** Particularly in more formal off-site work situations, a contract or an agreement can avoid misunderstandings and ensure that the organization and employee are on the same wavelength when it comes to the nitty-gritty details of the modified work arrangement. Items to be included in the contract include the hours the employee is expected to be available by phone or email, times the employee will need to report to the office, equipment that will be provided by the employer, safety issues, performance expectations, and training. See Chapter 4 for more information.

- **Training for both staff and managers:** Training of off-site staff and their managers is essential. Simply providing an employee with a computer and email is not enough. You may also want to consider providing training for those employees who will still be operating out of the office. The more you can do to thoroughly prepare the individuals involved in, or impacted by, flexible work arrangements, the greater your likelihood of success.

- **A method of evaluation:** How will you know if a modified work arrangement is successful? Establishing clear criteria to evaluate success against predetermined goals for both the employee and the organization will help determine if the time and effort invested is achieving desired results.

These are the foundational elements of establishing and maintaining effective and productive off-site working relationships, whether the people in those roles are employees or contractors. There is an important distinction between these two types of off-site workers that must be recognized and managed appropriately.

1.3 Understand the differences and similarities between off-site staff and gig workers (and why it's important)

Over the past decade there has been a steady increase in gig workers — people who don't work for a single employer but, instead, take on individual jobs, or gigs, from multiple employers. Uber and Lyft are two companies that have significantly driven this trend. Both hire drivers on a contract basis to provide ride services. Both have also come under scrutiny for how they interact with these supposed gig workers and whether they are actually contractors or need to be classified as traditional employees.

DoorDash has also joined the growing list of companies alleged to be misclassifying employees en masse. According to HRDive, the company was cited in June 2020 by San Francisco's district attorney who alleged the misclassification "was no mistake, but instead a calculated decision made to reduce the costs of doing business at the expense of the very workers providing the company's core service of delivery."

While some off-site staff may be members of what has come to be known as the "gig economy," not all staff who work off-site are gig workers. The distinction is important.

The Bureau of Labor Statistics refers to gig workers as "contingent" workers and defines them as: "people who do not expect their jobs to last or who reported that their jobs are temporary." These workers do not have "an implicit or explicit contract for continuing employment." This group of workers include those who may be called "independent contractors, on-call workers, temporary help agency workers, and workers provided by contract firms."

Why is the distinction important? Because employers are required to withhold taxes from employees' paychecks, but not required to do so for independent contractors, or gig workers who are required to pay these taxes themselves. While the criteria used to distinguish between the two categories of workers may seem, on the surface, to be fairly straightforward, employers are subject to stiff penalties and fines for misclassifying employees.

The IRS suggests three categories of considerations for determining whether staff should be classified as employees or whether they could be considered contractors, or gig workers: behavioral control, financial control, and relationship of the parties.

Behavioral control considers the amount of direction the employer exercises over how an individual does their work. The more control exerted, the more likely the individual should be classified as an employee. This would include:

- Direction as to when and where to work, type of tools to use, where to purchase supplies and services.

- How much detail is provided in terms of instructions to perform the work — the more detail, the greater likelihood the individual should be classified as an employee.

- How the work is evaluated. If only the end result, or deliverable, is evaluated, it's more likely the individual is a contractor.

- Training provided. Employees receive training, independent contractors generally do not.

Financial control considers the extent to which a business director controls financial aspects of an individual's work. For instance:

- Has the business made a significant investment in the equipment the individual uses?

- To what extent is the business reimbursing the individual for expenses related to their work? Independent contractors are less likely to be reimbursed than employees.

- To what extent does the individual have the opportunity for profit or loss? The more opportunity, the greater the likelihood the individual is an independent contractor.

- Are individuals free to seek additional business opportunities?

- What is the method of payment? Independent contractors are generally paid for the job and not by the hour or a salary.

- Relationship considerations relate to the interactions between the individual and the business or organization.

- Employees may receive benefits; independent contractors do not.

- With employees the relationship is considered to be somewhat "indefinite" contractors generally work for a specific period of time or to complete a specific project.

Similar guidelines are in place in Canada through the Canada Revenue Agency (CRA). Classification as self-employed means that individuals are not entitled to benefits under the Employment Insurance Act and also impact treatment under the Canada Pension Plan and Income Tax Act. Guidelines may vary based on the province or territory where the employee or contractor works. Similarly to the US, factors relate generally to the amount of control the employer exercises over how the individual does their work, whether the worker or the employer provides/pays for tools and equipment, and the individual's financial risk and opportunity for profit.

Given these criteria it's easy to understand why Uber and Lyft have been the subject of litigation attempting to change their classifications of drivers from contractors to employees.

Fines and penalties for misclassifying people as contractors instead of employees can be substantial. It's important for companies to seek advice from legal counsel to ensure they are classifying employees correctly.

2. Overcome Resistance from Managers and Employees

Not all employees or managers are going to eagerly embrace the concept of flexible work arrangements. Many employees, particularly those who have been on the job for a number of years and have grown comfortable with a particular way of working, may feel threatened by the changes that this flexibility may bring, primarily in terms of their ability to interact regularly with fellow employees in the manner in which they are accustomed.

Managers, in turn, may be concerned about their ability to supervise workers who are off-site based on previous experience that, in many cases, has involved only the supervision of employees working from a shared location.

The best way to respond to resistance is to understand where the resistance is coming from and what issues are creating concerns. Some of the concerns are predictable. There are a number of myths and misconceptions that you can clarify with employees.

For managers, concerns often center around these issues:

- "How can I supervise someone who is not in the office?"

- "How will I know if these employees are really working?"

- "Is it worth my time and effort to institute the guidelines and tracking systems necessary to make this work?"

These are legitimate questions, and it is important that you take the time to seriously listen to the concerns of your management staff and work out any problems.

The idea of supervising employees who are not physically accessible can be troublesome to managers who are used to having employees within view at all times. It is a different way of managing, but it is not an insurmountable problem. We will discuss methods of managing off-site staff in Chapter 9.

Another very legitimate concern that managers have about off-site employees is that they will be out of sight, and therefore out of mind. Managers are concerned that employees working away from the main physical location will miss out on critical information because they are no longer part of the informal communication channel, that their role on the team will be diminished, and their relationships with peers and managers will erode. That certainly can happen. Effective communication is a key component of any successful employment relationship. When managing off-site staff, the issues become more complex, but not insurmountable.

Managers aren't the only ones who may be resistant to these flexible arrangements, as we have seen. Employees may also have concerns, and their discontent, if not addressed, can hinder the success of these arrangements. Employee concerns often include:

- "It's not fair that employee X can work from home, but I can't."

- "Employee Y just wants to stay home with the kids."

- "I'm going to have to work harder to pick up the slack for these telecommuters."

- "How am I supposed to share information with people who aren't even around?"

There is an inherent benefit implied in the ability to work off-site, especially if that site is the employee's own home. Employees who are given this opportunity may elicit envy from their coworkers who, for whatever reasons, are not able to have the same flexibility. It is important to recognize the potential for internal conflict and jealousy. To minimize these conflicts, it is necessary to have very clearly identified, defined, and communicated criteria for the arrangement. Consistently adhering to these criteria can help to minimize conflict and jealousy among employees.

Frequent communication is an excellent way to overcome misconceptions that employees may have about their off-site peers. The concern that a new mother just wants to spend time at home with the baby, for instance, can be minimized by communicating the goals of the position and sharing information about the attainment of those goals. For example, if an off-site employee is part of a workgroup that is responsible for handling insurance claims, holding each employee (off-site and onsite) accountable for a specific number of claims can eliminate concerns about how time is being spent in a home location, for instance.

Resistance to change can be most readily overcome by implementing a well-defined system of policies and procedures with which everyone can become quickly familiar.

3. Resources Required: Equipment and Tools, Safety Considerations

The cost for setting up a home office for an employee can vary dramatically, as you might imagine. Different jobs will, of course, require different tools, and different companies have different capabilities. Who, then, should supply what? It seems that this, too, varies from business to business.

An important, and practical, consideration for companies is not to buy more technology than is needed. The business need should dictate the technology. Based on the work the employee will be doing, the company should determine the value of the investment to be made on their behalf.

Another concern for many organizations may be security. This is a concern that can be addressed and, in fact, many large financial institutions and healthcare organizations, two highly regulated industries where privacy and security are critical, manage remote workers regularly.

3.1 Office equipment and tools

Generally speaking, an employee working from an off-site location will need access to the same tools and equipment that allow him or her to be effective and productive in the office. Consider, for instance, the needs of an accountant. He or she would need access to a computer and the software required to do the job. Email, phone access, and videoconferencing capabilities would also likely be required.

A fax machine may not be necessary if the employee can send documents via email. Similarly, a photocopier may not be necessary if the remote worker has administrative support available through the corporate office. And, of course, the accountant would need a desk, office chair, filing space, and office supplies.

When considering the equipment necessary to establish an off-site workspace, it is important to achieve a balance between nice-to-have items and their impact on resources and productivity.

When providing equipment for employees, one important consideration is compatibility with the equipment at the main location. The employee's computer, for instance, should be powerful enough to accommodate the type of work he or she will be doing. Software programs should be the same type and version as coworkers will be using, and email programs should be compatible with those at the head office.

Who should pay for this equipment? For a number of reasons, it is best if the employer covers the costs. If you own the equipment, you have the right to tell the employee to use that equipment for business only. This can be particularly important if the employee will have access to sensitive company or customer information. Owning the equipment will also allow you to make decisions about the type of hardware, software, and other peripherals the employee should be using, and will ensure that your information-system staff are able to provide support for that equipment.

Michael Payne is the founder of AnywhereWorks which, as the name suggests, is a company that provides tools and resources to help companies manage communication and collaboration from anywhere. "We have always been a 'work anywhere' company," says Payne, "so our working practices, software and resources have always been geared towards allowing people to work outside the office." The keys to success, he says, are transparency, trust, and communication. But that requires the right tools and resources.

The majority of his team, he says, only need a desktop computer or laptop with a camera, internet connection, and space to work. "We really do subscribe to the idea that, with the right tools, you can create a digital workspace as good, if not better, than a physical office. However, we offer virtual receptionist services to businesses and for that people require a headset microphone, which we provide. Any other equipment requirements can be discussed on a case-by-case basis, but we're always open to suggestions. Anything that helps our team connect, collaborate, and thrive is a worthy investment," Payne says.

Staff are required to have a suitable internet connection — 2.5 Mbps download and 1.5 Mbps upload; each is given their own notebook computer. Because the company is paperless, he says, there is little need for more office supplies. "If somebody requires any other tools or supplies, however, we are open to discussion," he says.

In terms of tools, the staff get free access to the Anywhere app for internal communication and collaboration. It is, he says, "pivotal to helping our team manage projects and cooperate across departments." Using the app allows his staff to tag other team members, add media, and invite guests from outside the company to come in and collaborate.

At ServiceSource, says Patricia Elias, chief legal and people officer, staff were provided with some "office comforts" for their home such as multiple monitors, desk chairs, and standing desks, as applicable. This, she says enabled employees to set up a more permanent home working environment which is critical to long-term success. Staff feedback has been very positive, she says, "with lots of gratitude for us putting the safety of our employees first." Staff quickly moved to remote work environments during COVID-19 and Elias anticipates they'll remain there through the end of 2020.

Fixr.com, a home remodeling information website conducted a survey of home design experts to determine how people were adapting to working from home and recommendations for better productivity. Their key findings:

- Isolation from household distractions is the best way to increase productivity at home.

- Desk lamps are the most recommended task lighting source.

- Noise-canceling headphones are the most recommended way to reduce noise.

- Soft white is the color most recommended to help increase productivity in the home office.

Sometimes "little things" can also mean a lot. For instance, Heinrich Long shares an experience he had with his staff during the COVID-19 crisis. Long is privacy expert at Restore Privacy, an online privacy and security resource center. After two months of remote working, he says, the company issued a survey to all staff to collect feedback on working from home and whether improvements could be made.

"As a result, we offered each member of staff a coffee subscription whereby ground coffee is delivered to their home on a weekly basis," Long says. "This was a huge morale booster for employees who were complaining that personal costs had risen slightly as a result of working from home. The coffee subscription was a low-cost way of showing staff that we care!"

When employers provide equipment, it's important to ensure that employees understand that the employer owns that equipment and that they will be required to return it if the employment relationship ends. That can be done at the point of hire, or onboarding, as part of the process of having all employees fill out required paperwork.

3.2 Safety considerations

There are a variety of safety issues to be considered when setting up a home office, and, of course, there is the issue of who should take responsibility for ensuring the safety of the home office.

Employers are responsible for employee safety. The problem is that in an era of virtual work, the bounds of that responsibility are very unclear. If an employee is injured due to an electrical shock because of a frayed cord on the computer in his or her home office, which was supplied by the employer, is the employer at fault? Most reasonable adults would say, "Probably." But is the employer at fault if that same employee slipped and fell on the way to the bathroom while working at home? Most reasonable adults would say, "Probably not."

There are obviously no easy answers. The boundaries between work and home are becoming increasingly blurred. The solution is to develop very clear policies and guidelines regarding safety issues of employees working from home.

Eric J. Stark, Esq., is an associate attorney at Pond Lehocky where he concentrates his practice on advocating for injured workers. "Workers' compensation is a benefit provided to employees who sustain injuries while in the course and scope of their employment; any time they are performing tasks for the benefit of their employer," says Stark. "As many people have transitioned from working at the office to working from home, they are still susceptible to injuries," he says. "One challenge in this regard is the fact that, when working from home, the employee is in the course and scope of employment potentially longer than he or she is when working at a fixed location," he says. Common injuries related to telecommuting, he says, can include:

- Carpal tunnel syndrome

- Overextension

- Back injuries

- Pinched nerves

- Eye strain

- Slips/trips/falls

When employees are working from home and sustain an injury, Stark says, "there is a question as to whether or not the employee was still within the course and scope of employment at the time of the injury." That determination, he says, is based on a number of factual and legal factors, but it's important for employees who believe they were injured while working remotely to document everything and contact their employer immediately.

Employers, Stark says, should communicate regularly with employees about safety issues. "Providing safety tips, updates to policies and procedures are great first steps," he says. "Regular safety meetings should still be held even virtually in order to ensure that the company is still providing a safe working environment regardless of the circumstances."

Employees, in turn, are responsible for setting up a safe workspace and for ensuring that they keep open lines of communication with their employer in terms of any risk factors that they are uniquely susceptible to given their home environment. How can employers know that they have done that and that they are continuing to maintain a safe environment?

Employers are entitled to inspect an employee's workspace and working arrangements, even when they're working from home, says Stark, and they should be doing that "at least periodically," he says. "That will also ensure communication between both parties and an appropriate assessment and mitigation of risk."

The Occupational Safety and Health Administration (OSHA), says Trey Dean, owner of LowRisq.com and an OSHA Authorized Instructor in General Industry and Construction, does not inspect home offices, and is only concerned with home-based businesses that are involved in the manufacture of goods. He points to guidance contained in the federal regulation: CPL 2-0.125, Home Based Worksites. Ultimately, he says, "OSHA expects that the home-based office or worksite is made safe by the employer."

Like Stark, Dean recommends that employers physically inspect home offices; he suggests they do this every six months. In addition, he says that employers should "ensure that there is a mutually agreed-upon work-from-home policy that clearly outlines expectations to include inspections and insurance, if applicable. "The employee must give consent for a home office inspection and this should be clearly outlined."

In cases where the individual is classified as a contractor, these inspections would not be done. The individual would be responsible for his or her own personal safety, workspace, and insurance coverage.

4. Lessons from the Trenches

Hackler Flynn & Associates is a California law firm that was set up for remote work years before COVID-19. It's a primarily paperless office. Employees use their own computers and phones for remote work. However, they are supported by staff with equipment at the office. If employees need additional equipment at home, they make a request for that equipment. The firm supplies a "full suite of tools to successfully work remotely," which includes:

- Secure web-based time keeping

- Secure web-based document management

- Web-based phone application

- Video conferencing application

- Secure web-based HR

- Tech support

"Employees working from home must designate a workspace that is maintained in safe condition, free from hazards," says Cynthia Flynn, Esq., founder and managing partner of the firm. "We also require that employees take all precautions necessary to secure company information and equipment in their homes and to prevent authorized access to any company system or information. Employees must password protect access on their home computers, laptops, and cell phones to keep work information confidential. Further, employees will set their cell phones to lock automatically after one minute of inactivity and their home/laptop computers to lock automatically after five minutes of inactivity."

Employees are offered a stipend for phone and internet connections and, if there are any other expenses, they would place them on their monthly expense report for reimbursement. This is not only a company policy, says Flynn, but also the law under California Labor Code Section 2802 which requires employers to reimburse all reasonable and "necessary" expenses that employees incur "in direct consequence of discharging their job duties." It's important, she says, for all employers to be familiar with the laws that may apply to providing equipment to remote workers.

Employers must also consider OSHA guidelines, she says. "OSHA currently does not enforce federal regulations for employers to follow when their employees work from home," says Flynn. "However, an OSHA Compliance Directive exists for home-based worksites, or areas of an employee's personal residence where the employee performs work for the employer." This means, she says, "that an employer must make sure that any equipment provided to workers is in good condition. Poor equipment can lead to unnecessary work-related accidents, e.g., fires."

Chapter 4

POLICIES AND PROCEDURES

According to a Zenefits report, "The State of Flexible Work Arrangements," while 67% of respondents indicated that their employer offered some type of flexible work, 58% said that the company they worked for either didn't have an official policy or they were unsure about whether such a policy existed. Employees from larger companies (301–500 employees) were more likely to report having policies related to remote work (53%); those at smaller companies (1–20 employees) were the least likely to report having a formal policy (26%).

Employers with employees who are working from home, or other remote locations, need to have policies in place to ensure that both they and their employees are protected.

Mary Moakley, JD, is a legal editor with XpertHR, an information services firm that helps organizations achieve greater efficiency, reduce risk, and increase employee engagement says: "An employer should set forth its expectations with respect to attendance, availability, productivity, supervision and off-site work. Policies and procedures, employee handbook statements and any associated acknowledgments should be available to employees in order to decide whether to explore remote work as an option. Prior to engaging in remote work, an employer should require a telecommuting agreement that is specific to the employee's situation, complies with all applicable laws, and clarifies any issues that may arise, including specific regarding company equipment and property, reimbursement of costs, off-the-clock work, and tax implications."

Supervisors, says Moakley, "need to continue to manage employees and to ensure that they continue to be productive. Leveraging technology to derive measurable data on a remote worker's performance may yield more quantitative, objective measures of performance than traditional observation."

Policies and procedures need to be applied uniformly.

Moakley advises that supervisors "should guard against making any assumptions as to whether an employee would be more or less productive when working remotely." She provides some examples:

- Denying an older worker the opportunity to work from home because of assumed technical challenges. For instance, assuming an employee nearing retirement age would not be technically savvy enough to deal with computer issues off-site, or would not be able to or interested in learning how to use communication tools such as Zoom.

- Denying a young mother the opportunity based on an assumption that she will be distracted by her children during work hours could lead to inconsistent opportunities for employees in protected classes and, consequently, a higher likelihood of discrimination claims.

"To ensure that remote working assignments are made in a fair manner, an employer may designate certain positions or departments as eligible for flexible work arrangements based on specific job requirements and business goals, and ensure that any decisions with respect to placements are reviewed by at least two managers and human resources," Oakley recommends.

There are myriad details to consider when establishing relationships or arrangements with employees who will work from off-site locations. It can be the little things that often create the most frustration and require the most effort, such as coming up with an appropriate contract for the program, dealing with performance measurement, or figuring out how to deal with certain legal issues that affect the employee/employer relationship.

The rest of this chapter discusses the kinds of policies and procedures that you will have to implement in your business to make these arrangements work most effectively. See the downloadable forms kit (URL at the back of the book) for sample policies, agreements, and guidelines that have made flexible arrangements, as well as formal telecommuting programs, a success for other organizations.

In organizations with multiple locations that may require the supervision of employees at various sites, overall organizational policies generally apply, with some exceptions that might be specific to each area's specific characteristics. For instance, one site may have a large fitness facility, while another may have a walking path; one site may have a cafeteria, another may not; access to the building may vary, etc. Aside from specific physical differences that may require minor variations in policy, the broad organizational policies will apply to all employees, regardless of where they are physically located.

Other types of flexible arrangements telecommuting programs, for instance will require specific policies to address the issues related to use of company property, communication requirements, and more.

The more specific and clear you can be about the requirements and processes for your nontraditional work arrangements, the fewer misunderstandings or problems you will encounter. Considering policy and procedure issues before you receive requests from employees will help you make good decisions based on the needs of your organization.

1. Policy Statement

It is very important to take the time to develop a policy specific to your organization's unique needs. While various sample policies are available and may be useful as a starting point, your policy should be customized to the culture and operations of your organization and should provide a summary of your organization's position regarding flexible work arrangements. The following are key elements that should be included:

- A statement that the flexible work arrangement is at the employer's discretion and that the employer/manager is responsible for determining when/where work will be performed in accordance with business needs.

- Criteria for identifying eligible positions and incumbents (e.g., tenure with the organization, minimum performance level, job types).

- Terms and conditions of the arrangement (e.g., types of flexible options offered, communication requirements, ability to alter arrangement at management's discretion).

- Core hours and a clear system and guidelines for reporting hours worked (or other measurements). In addition, employers should include language indicating that unauthorized work is prohibited and a process/procedure for the approval of overtime hours.

- Any specific communication requirements (e.g., "face time" in the office, conference call, or meeting attendance expectations, etc.).

- Equipment (e.g., what type will be required, who will purchase, and who will support/insure).

- Workers' compensation and safety statement notifying employees that any injuries sustained at home in the course of work need to be reported, as well as an explanation of the mechanism for reporting.

- Confidential information and expectations for its protection from unauthorized observers or use.

- How performance will be evaluated and its relevance to continued flexible arrangement.

- The policy should make it clear that the ability to work under a flexible arrangement is not an entitlement or perk, but a business imperative that will be monitored and modified based on business need.

You may wish to specify the supervisor's role in determining the details of these off-site arrangements. For example, you might discuss the supervisor's right to determine the length, duration, and timeframes of the arrangement (i.e., how many days per week are appropriate), and/or the supervisor's evaluation schedule and the criteria by which the employee's performance will be judged.

You may also wish to address specific requirements of the program, such as:

- Requiring a signed agreement for all participants in a formal telecommuting program.

- Requiring training as a prerequisite to working in an off-site capacity.

- For employees working from home locations, you might also consider including in your policy statement some discussion of what is not acceptable. For example, you might state that working from home is not a solution for care of dependents.

Despite the importance of having policies and procedures to ensure compliance, fair treatment and mutual understanding, making these relationships work doesn't have to be overly complex, says Andrew Meadows, senior vice president at Ubiquity Retirement + Savings in San Francisco where about 85% of the organization's 85 employees work from home. At Ubiquity, he says, the rules for working from home are really quite simple. The company has three rules, he says:

- Overcommunicate about taking breaks, your schedule, etc.

- Be available for impromptu meetings and discussions.

- Get your job done.

With those rules, he said, employees can manage themselves. "We like to call it 'freedom with accountability.'"

2. Selection Criteria

Specific selection criteria will help you avoid discrimination charges arising out of claims of favoritism. Criteria may include such traits as self-motivation, strong communication skills, and the ability to work independently. Selection criteria might also include length-of-service requirements and consideration based on employee evaluations (e.g., an employee may work in an off-site role if he or she has received satisfactory or higher ratings on performance evaluations for the past X years). In addition, selection criteria should include factors related to the types of jobs or tasks that can be performed off-site. The more specific you are as to what criteria are acceptable, the more smoothly your program will run.

3. Expectations/Responsibilities of Off-site Employees

Your policy and WFH agreements should outline the expectations that the company has of its off-site staff, detailing as much as possible, from furnishings to security issues.

3.1 Work hours

One of the benefits that telecommuting employees receive is flexibility in hours of work. But that flexibility must still be tied to the needs of the workplace including the needs of coworkers and customers (internal and external). Being available to take phone calls or respond to email messages may be critical for some positions, but not others. For example, an employee working in a virtual call center operation and answering calls at home would need to be available to take calls from customers at specific, established times throughout the day. A computer programmer working at home, however, may not have the same access requirements. Each position will vary, but for each position, you should very clearly indicate the hours you expect the employee to be working.

The requirements of each individual position will determine the hours in which the work needs to take place. Certain positions (inbound telephone sales representatives, for instance) may be required to be available during certain hours of the day, while others (computer programmers, for example) may not have such restrictions.

3.2 Work assignments

What will the employee be responsible for? Existing job descriptions are a good starting point and may be sufficient to cover the actual work performed. In addition, though, you will want to consider:

- How work assignments will be provided.

- If employees will be required to meet or contact the supervisor on a regularly scheduled basis to discuss assignments, or if assignments will be made as they occur.

3.3 Employer's right to inspect workplace

Companies should clearly indicate if and when the company or manager will have the right to inspect or visit the employee's off-site work location. For instance, you may want to reserve the right to access the home office for purposes of safety inspections, accident investigations, equipment audits, or other business-related matters. Visits are usually based on reasonable notice, generally 24 hours, or less, if agreed to by the employee.

Today's technology, of course, allows for these types of inspections to be done remotely through video walkthroughs which can be the preferred route to minimize potential coronavirus exposure.

3.4 Privacy and confidentiality

Employees working from their homes, particularly those who are connected to the home office electronically, present a certain amount of security risk for your organization. Consider having these employees sign confidentiality agreements. Indicate in the agreement whether or not the employee may use computer equipment for non-work-related activities. Security procedures must be discussed in detail, with emphasis on the need for strict adherence to the procedures.

3.5 Performance measurement

Off-site employees and their managers should work together to come up with applicable quantitative measures of performance. These measures should be documented as part of the agreement and should clearly indicate what the expectations are of the employee in terms of quantity and quality of work, as well as how often and in what manner the employee's performance will be measured.

3.6 Salary and benefits

What will the employee's pay be? Will the employee be paid by the hour or have a salary? What benefits will apply? Will salary or pay be impacted for employees who work out of their homes? It's a question that has been raised. Mark Zuckerberg, for example, has said that salaries may be lower for those who live in a location where cost of living is dramatically lower. That may, or may not, make sense for your company, but it's an important issue to consider and address through your pay practices.

3.7 Overtime

One of the concerns that many employers have about allowing employees to work from home is that they cannot be monitored. The potential exists for more time to be devoted to a project than might be necessary. One way to address this concern, particularly with hourly employees, is to have a policy that overtime will not be allowed unless approved by the supervisor.

Another is to establish clear expectations about productivity. This is, of course, easier to do when you have a number of employees whose work output can be compared.

3.8 Equipment and supplies

Will the employer provide equipment for the employee? Will the employee be allowed to use his or her own equipment? If the employee can use his or her own equipment, will he or she be compensated for that use? Will repairs to employee-owned equipment be paid by the employer? Be specific in outlining your equipment policies, addressing issues such as confidentiality, personal use, upgrades, and return of company equipment upon termination.

This section of the agreement should outline, in detail, the equipment and supplies that will be provided by the company and those that will be the responsibility of the off-site employee. Standards, where applicable, should also be included (i.e., requirements for certain types of furniture based on safety considerations, etc.). Indicate, also, whether and to what extent the employee will be responsible for maintenance and repair of equipment, what the employer's role will be, and how repairs will be handled (i.e., equipment will need to be brought into the office or the company will send a repair person to the employee's home location). Again, be as specific as possible to avoid any employee confusion or dissatisfaction.

3.9 Insurance

You should verify what type of coverage is afforded the off-site employee based on your existing insurance policy, and decide whether the employee will be responsible for providing any additional coverage. The employee should indemnify the company from any injuries claimed by any third parties and should be required to maintain appropriate insurance coverage for these types of claims.

3.10 Termination of agreement

An "exit strategy" should be outlined at the onset of any special agreement allowing an employee to work in an off-site setting or establishing a telecommuting arrangement. The agreement should include a section dealing with the potential termination of the agreement by the company, manager, or employee. It should detail the situation(s) under which the agreement might be terminated (e.g., inability to perform work duties as outlined in the agreement). It should also discuss the employee's options upon termination of the agreement. Can the employee maintain the position in-house, can he or she apply for another in-house position, or is the employee terminated from the company? The termination agreement must also address the disposition of any company equipment that has been purchased for the employee's use at home.

3.11 Employment-at-will disclaimer

A remote or alternative work arrangement agreement does not constitute a contract of employment. The agreement should indicate, as applicable, that the employee remains employed on an at-will basis and can be terminated with or without cause and with or without notice.

4. Communicate Policies and Policy Changes

Whether outlined in a specific telecommuting policy, contract, or agreement, or included as part of existing policies and procedures that impact all workers, companies should be certain that they are providing clear and specific written documentation of the understanding between them and any off-site staff. Policies should address all of the details that will impact how the arrangement works, how the employee will interact with the head office, and what the company's expectations are for the relationship. (**Note:** These expectations will serve as a key part of training for off-site staff, as well as their managers.)

If a separate policy is being created to address an off-site employee's unique situation, or as part of a formal telecommuting program, include a statement in the policy document to indicate that these employees will also be required to abide by all other existing company policies and procedures, except as they differ from specific items as outlined in the agreement.

5. Lessons from the Trenches

Kent Lewis is president and founder of Anvil, a marketing firm in Portland, Oregon. He supervises a team of nine digital marketing staff members who do work related to search engine optimization (SEO), paid search, and social media advertising, while also working remotely himself.

While the group wasn't remote prior to COVID-19, he says that the transition was not difficult. One of the biggest adjustments, he says, has been creating intentional check-ins with the team. These used to be monthly, but are now done via email and video conferencing on a weekly basis.

"We've modified all meetings to be virtual, which has definitely lost some off the energy, collaboration and creativity provided by face-to-face interactions." That, he says, is a primary reason that the team wasn't remote prior to the impact of the virus.

For team members, the biggest adjustment was finding a space to work from home. Many borrowed chairs and monitors from the office, he says. The need to find a dedicated workspace at home, he says, is something he wished he'd known about earlier to help make the transition easier. "It doesn't have to be a full-blown office, but it should be a private room with a desk and chair at least."

Lewis' priorities have shifted as he's moved from direct to remote management. "I feel more connected with my staff now than prior, as my responsibilities have shifted and I've elected to focus first on my employees, second on my clients, and last on new business, marketing. That is an inverse of my priorities prior," he says.

Communication is really key to making these remote relationships work, he says. "Based on my experience, I recommend creating regular check-ins, both manager to employee and peer-to-peer. We already had a weekly staff and strategy meeting on our calendars

Mondays and Wednesdays respectively. We added a virtual Friday at Four Happy Hour video conference and it's been an amazing way to connect and end the week strong." He's also added an email check-in with all employees weekly, in addition to monthly one-on-one meetings, which are now done via video conference.

Technology helps. The team uses project management tools such as Basecamp or Asana, collaboration tools like Slack, and video conferencing and file-sharing tools such as UberConference, Zoom, or WebEx.

The key to ensuring great communication, which is a must-have, is consistency, he says. Remote work relationships can work, but they require a different sort of focus than when interacting with employees in face-to-face work environments.

Chapter 5

THOSE YOU KNOW – CHARACTERISTICS OF SUCCESSFUL REMOTE WORKERS AND SELECTION CRITERIA

Employers, managers, and supervisors tend to be far more comfortable allowing existing employees to work from home or some other remote location than they are hiring people, sight unseen, to work from afar. Those they know, and have established relationships with, represent less risk for them because they feel they can more accurately assess their ability to work independently, their productivity, and their commitment to their job and the company.

But even when potential remote workers are known commodities, not all will be able to excel at remote work. When considering whether or not to offer an employee the opportunity to work from home, it's important to understand the traits of successful remote workers.

1. Who Thrives, Survives, or Dives?

Just as some jobs are more appropriate for off-site arrangements than others, certain employees are more suited to working in these situations than other employees. Some employees may not even be interested. You may be surprised to find, in fact, that a number of your staff prefer the camaraderie and sense of team that the workplace holds. Other employees may simply realize that they are not self-motivated enough to be productive away from the traditional workplace. Still others have home situations that might make it inconvenient or untenable for them to work there. And many people will find it difficult to maintain a division between home life and work life when home and work share a location.

2. Traits of Successful Remote Workers

A successful employee is successful whether he or she works from home, at a branch location, or at the head office. Assuming that the job is appropriate for off-site work, you probably already have a good idea of how your employee will perform. Yet there are some specific skills that require particular emphasis in off-site positions.

On the downloadable forms kit (see back of book for instructions for downloading) is a useful summary of the traits found to be common among successful telecommuters, drawn (with grateful permission) from the ALLearnatives assessment tool.

Successful off-site workers share a number of important traits which include:

- Staying connected with coworkers and the boss. This requires a certain amount of proactive communication. Rather than waiting for the phone to ring or for the email message to arrive, successful off-site employees take the initiative to stay connected.

- Being well organized. Many employees who move from the traditional work setting to an off-site location, particularly a home location, come from environments in which they had ready access to administrative staff. When working alone, that access may be limited or nonexistent.

- Getting out of the house. Working off-site doesn't mean burrowing. Successful remote employees take advantage of opportunities to network with coworkers, peers, and other colleagues by making lunch dates, being active in professional associations, and generally staying in touch.

- Separating home from work. When working from home, it can be difficult to avoid the lure of personal tasks — such as washing clothes or taking care of children and pets. It's important to learn how to establish clear boundaries between home and work.

- Making technology their friend. Technology has made working from remote locations in virtually any setting possible and popular. The many tools such as email, group scheduling, and teleconferencing make it easy to stay connected, regardless of physical and geographic barriers.

- Knowing when to take a break. A common downfall of working outside the traditional work environment, according to those who have experienced it, is the tendency to work too much!

Certain employees may prove to be ill-suited to working in an environment where they have no direct supervision and, potentially, limited contact with others. They may include employees who have a high need for social interaction, are easily distracted by outside demands and interruptions, need the office setting to provide an environment conducive to work, and do not have adequate childcare arrangements or supportive family situations.

Working in nontraditional environments — or at remote locations — is not an option that should be available to all employees. Your decision on whether to place an employee in a branch or remote location, or to allow that employee to work from home in a telecommuting arrangement will depend on the demands and characteristics of the job as well as the personal traits of the employee. Selection criteria should be carefully considered and clearly outlined in your policies and contract, as appropriate.

3. Assess Candidates

How can you determine whether employees will be suited to this type of work? Your own observation of their performance during their employment with your company can certainly provide some indications. In addition, you will want to spend some time speaking with the employee and exploring the pros and cons of alternative work arrangements to provide both of you with a sense of whether or not these options will be appropriate.

Using an assessment tool, like the remote-work readiness assessment from JotForm, in the selection of candidates for remote work can be another effective way to avoid any charges of arbitrariness. Such a tool can provide both the employee and his or her manager with an indication of readiness or appropriateness for working from home.

4. Potential Pitfalls

Your company and management staff should be aware of some common issues that may arise when selecting staff for off-site work, or approving such requests.

4.1 It just doesn't work with the employee

One of the greatest potential pitfalls involved in selecting employees to work remotely or in off-site locations is choosing the wrong employee. Fortunately, it's a pitfall that can be overcome. Not all employees will thrive in these roles, regardless of how careful the selection process was, how thoroughly the employee was trained and prepared, and how exceptional the support from the workplace is. Sometimes it just doesn't work out. That's okay. In your policy or contract, recognize the possibility of failure and clearly indicate what happens when the situation does not prove to be successful. Address such issues as how long the trial period will be; what criteria will be used to determine the success of the arrangement; whether the employee will be able to terminate the arrangement and under what circumstances; whether the employee's manager will be able to terminate the arrangement and under what circumstances; whether the employee be able to return to his or her traditional position and in what instances might this not be possible?

Both manager and employee should thoroughly review the potential for the arrangement to prove unacceptable before the alternative work assignment begins.

4.2 It's not fair!

The ability to work from home is frequently viewed as a benefit by employees particularly by those who do not have this option. This is a very real issue and one that should be considered and addressed.

Having clearly established criteria and a well-defined process for the selection of off-site employees can help prevent problems related to perceived inequities or favoritism. It will also be important to be fair and consistent in your decisions to let staff work from home. Whatever your criteria for identifying employees who will have the opportunity to work from home, you need to be consistent.

4.3 My manager won't let me!

Managers need to be receptive to the concept of telecommuting. Problems can develop if one manager allows his or her employees to telecommute and another manager with similar types of employees doesn't. Offering the option to work from home should be an organizational decision and a policy should be written that all managers and supervisors should be required to follow.

Again, establishing criteria — both for the types of jobs and the types of individuals — for who can work from home, and applying these criteria consistently can help avoid frustration among employees and feelings of inequity.

Remote work isn't a "special favor" to be offered to employees. It should be a strategic company decision to leverage the many benefits of remote work for the company and employees.

5. Lessons from the Trenches

Alix Rubin is the owner of Rubin Employment Law, based in Fairfield, New Jersey. Rubin thinks employers will need to focus on training managers to work with remote teams in a post-COVID environment. So far, since the pandemic hit, employers have had a range of experiences with remote teams. She recommended putting a structure in place and managing the communications with employees daily. "You need to agree on how and how often you and your employees are checking in with each other," she advises.

"Whether you use Zoom or a product like Webex, it's the communication itself that is key to successfully managing remote teams," she says. The manager needs to make the effort to see the person.

If you agree to a check-in twice daily, it needs to happen. And the check-in can be brief. A group meeting, or huddle, as they are often called, can be ten minutes or less to help employees avoid feelings of isolation. "We all need to feel a part of the team," she says.

Rubin recommends that employees who work from home sign a document that specifies all WFH policies, and that it's posted/printed in the Employee Handbook. A signature indicates that each affected employee has read and acknowledged the WFH policies, Rubin says. "Those signed agreements are important in case any discipline is needed."

For confidentiality reasons, employers may prefer that remote employees use a dedicated office for their workspace. But that is not always possible, she says, and employers were in no position to dictate such a requirement when employees were quickly sent home to work in mid-March after the Coronavirus pandemic was declared by the World Health Organization. However, she says, employers "can require a space that is as free as possible from distractions."

Rubin relays a funny story about how her husband, even though she was logged into a Zoom call from her home office, "walked in and stood there talking to me while my mic was on. Fortunately, I was able to shut the mic off quickly and wave him off."

"As employees, we all need to find ways to set boundaries with our families while we are working from home," she says. It's tougher, though, when a family includes toddlers who are too young to read the "Mommy is working" note on the office door.

Based on client questions, Rubin isn't certain if most companies will allow WFH activities to continue in a post-COVID environment. Much will depend on the individual industry and how easy it is to work from home. Based on anecdotal discussions on a Zoom association meeting for attorneys that she attended recently, Rubin said many were not planning to head back to the office until fall. It's very easy to store documents in the cloud. For that reason, she thinks some companies will be much more likely to set up WFH opportunities for their employees.

"We just need to be willing to accept preferences from employees who like the best of both worlds — some work at home and time at the office," she says.

A question that all employers need to ask themselves: How do I monitor productivity with pre-COVID systems? She suggests that some companies may need to make technology investments.

Ultimately, though, Rubin believes employees will need to trust their employees. "If you had a problem employee in the office, you likely will have a problem employee working from home," she says.

Chapter 6

THOSE YOU DON'T – RECRUITING EMPLOYEES FOR TELECOMMUTING POSITIONS

Most organizations that use telecommuters select them from their existing workforce. Face it: That's the least risky thing to do. They are familiar with these people. They've proven their worth, their commitment, and their efficiency.

But what if you really don't have anybody on staff that you feel would be suitable for a remote position? Worse, what if you're looking for certain skills or experience that just don't seem to exist in your geographic area? Or, as seems to be the case more often these days, what if your organization isn't a brick-and-mortar facility and you don't really care where your employees live, as long as they can do the job?

Today's technology and ease of communication around the globe makes it quick, convenient, and cost-effective to recruit employees from anywhere. The COVID-19 situation has focused recruiters, HR professionals, and hiring managers on creativity when it comes to reaching out to potential employees and taking them through the acquisition process often remotely. Jobvite sought input from more than 200 recruiters to learn how their talent teams were adapting their approaches. One of the biggest findings was the integration of video into the recruiting process, 73% of recruiters indicated that they used video and online meetings to facilitate the onboarding process. Additional findings:

- 84% of talent acquisition teams are adapting their processes to work remotely

- 46% of respondents are doing more social posting to advertise jobs to recruit new talent, including on LinkedIn, Facebook, and Instagram

- 58% of respondents are using social channels to promote their employer brand and connect with talent

- 80% of respondents are using video in the interview process

- 61% of respondents are using video as part of the screening process

- 55% of respondents are making more phone calls than before

- 27% of respondents are using more texting to communicate with candidates following an offer letter

- 8% of respondents are using chatbots to facilitate initial candidate screening

Zoom is by far the most popular videoconferencing software being used for conducting job interviews, according to research from ResumeGo, a national résumé writing service, with 43% of respondents indicating that they use Zoom; the next most popular tool is GoogleMeet/Hangouts (19%). Interviews generally last between 30 minutes and an hour (48% of respondents). Interestingly, while 52% of respondents say they prefer candidates to wear business casual attire for interviews, only 4% prefer formal attire, 44% say it doesn't matter to them.

Unfortunately, while recruiters are increasingly turning to videoconferencing tools for interviews, the process isn't always smooth. They observe candidates running into problems with videoconferencing software (36%), loud background noise (27%), being late to the interview (16%), poor audio quality (9%), poor video quality (5%), and 7% do say they've encountered issues with "improper attire."

But, while many of the approaches being used to find and engage with candidates are shifting in a virtual world, the steps in the hiring process remain very much the same.

1. Steps in the Hiring Process

Whether advertising in the local paper, running an ad online, or "trolling" for employees on a social media site such as LinkedIn, the hiring process you use for finding remote workers will be much the same as for any employee.

These steps include:

- Identifying the need for a new position, or the need to add one, or more new employees to an existing position

- Creating or updating the job description

- Creating a position description

- Creating a job requisition

- Advertising the position

- Evaluating applicants and selecting potential employees

- Conducting interviews

- Evaluating interviewees and making a selection

- Extending an offer

- Onboarding the new employee

In the new environment that employers now find themselves in since COVID-19, whenever the need for a new employee arises, it can be a good idea to consider whether that position is one that would allow for remote work. The job description can be a good starting point. So can information from the exiting employee (if this is not a new position) and his or her manager or supervisor. Together a determination can be made about whether the position is one that —

- must be done remotely,

- could be done either remotely or onsite, or

- can only be done onsite.

As we've discussed, the determination of whether a position or employee may be remote opens up new, and additional, opportunities for recruitment.

2. Position Requirements

As with any position, your first step in hiring a telecommuter will be determining the requirements of the position. This will not only help you make an informed decision, but will also help narrow your choices in terms of recruitment vehicles. Before you begin your search, you should consider the following:

- **Education:** What level of education is necessary to perform effectively in the position? High school? College? Special training? Will job performance require any type of special certificate or license?

- **Experience:** How much previous, related experience should a new employee have? Will training be offered on the job? Experience and education requirements are often tied together; for example, "Bachelor's degree plus a minimum of three years' experience in the field."

- **Personality requirements:** As discussed in Chapter 4, there are specific personality traits that differentiate those who will perform effectively as telecommuters from those who will not be successful in this role.

As you put together your list of requirements, make sure that each is specifically job related to avoid claims or charges of discrimination. Don't make these job determinations in a vacuum. Ask other members of the organization for their perspectives.

Be specific. Communication is a critical element in any telecommuting relationship, and it starts during recruitment. You should have a very clear understanding of what the job will entail and the specific requirements of the position. Job descriptions and job specifications are two tools that can greatly help you in this process.

The job description provides a written record of the qualifications required for the position and outlines how the job relates to others in the company. It should include:

- Position title

- Salary or pay grade

- Department

- Who the position reports to

- Hours of availability required

- Job summary

- Major responsibilities or tasks

- Qualifications

- Relation of the position to others in the company

The job description should be organized in such a way that it indicates not only the responsibilities involved, but also the relative importance of these responsibilities. The job description should also indicate how the remote employee will interact with colleagues, and should discuss other issues related to the employment relationship. Within the broad categories mentioned above, you will want to include such information as the following:

- Extent of authority exercised over the position

- Level of complexity of the duties performed

- Amount of internal and external contact (including any requirements for onsite meetings)

- Amount of access to confidential information

- Amount of independent judgment required

- Amount of pressure involved in the job

- Type of equipment used (and how that equipment will be purchased and maintained)

- Working conditions (including expectations for the home office environment)

- Terms of employment

Job specifications are another useful tool in the recruitment process. Job specifications describe the personal qualifications that are required for a job and include any special conditions of employment. In the case of telecommuting, this may include such things as required hours of availability and responsibility for maintaining equipment.

Some key questions to ask yourself as you are preparing a position description include:

- What is the purpose of the job?
- What day-to-day duties are performed?
- How is the position supervised?
- What other positions receive supervision from this position?
- How much, or how little, control is exercised over this position?
- What machines or equipment must be operated?
- What types of records need to be kept by this position?
- To what extent is this position involved in analysis and planning?
- What internal and external contacts are required of this position?
- What verbal, numerical, or mechanical aptitudes are required?

One of the real benefits of hiring individuals to work remotely is that they don't have to live anywhere near your business. Your hiring pool is infinitely large. But the sheer size of this pool can also present a disadvantage when it comes to recruiting. Where do you begin?

Today's hiring managers and recruiters have a wide range of tools to turn to when looking for candidates. Increasingly, they're turning to those tools to help expedite the recruiting process, especially when hiring staff for remote positions.

Jobvite research published in its Remote Recruiting Report offers some insights into the current state of recruitment for remote job candidates:

- An overwhelming majority of talent acquisition teams, 84%, are adapting their processes to work remotely amid the COVID-19 environment.
- 46% of respondents are using social media posting more to recruit new talent.

- 61% of the recruiters surveyed indicated that they are using video as part of the screening process; 80% are using it in the interview process. Using video to screen candidates can eliminate unqualified candidates quickly, and accelerate connections with the best candidates even more quickly.

- Only 27% of the recruiters surveyed indicated that they are using more texting to communicate with candidates following an offer letter. Texting is an easy, quick way to communicate with candidates. On average, candidates see a text within 90 seconds, as opposed to an email, which is 90 minutes on average.

- 73% of those surveyed indicated that they are using video and online meetings to facilitate the onboarding process.

Here we take a look at these opportunities and how you can best leverage them to reach out to and engage potential candidates for remote positions, no matter where they happen to be located.

3. Your Website As a Recruiting Tool

Your website can be a great, ongoing, source of job inquiries and applicants. If you have a website already, consider adding a section detailing your vacant positions. Make your website user-friendly by offering job seekers the ability to search by keywords, location, job title, or pay. Include the option to apply for positions or submit résumés online. Again, being specific and detailed is important. Consider these listings your one opportunity to attract the attention of interested applicants.

Of course, simply including job listings on your site isn't enough to generate response. You need to make sure that potential job seekers know that this information is available. That means promoting your site. Promote your website through traditional communication channels by ensuring that the web address is included prominently on traditional print media (e.g., direct mail, notices on statements, etc.). Include your web address in all your traditional employment advertisements. It's really a matter of being consistent about your marketing and using a number of different vehicles to market.

Most important, make sure that your listings are up to date, and that you're responsive to the inquiries that you do receive.

4. The Internet As a Recruiting Tool

The internet offers a wide range of options for employers looking for employees of all kinds. Many sites cater specifically to employers hiring remote workers. VirtualVocations.com, for instance, is a very large network for remote workers and the employers that hire them. It was started in February 2007 with the sole purpose of providing legitimate and diverse remote work employment positions to those interested in working from home; positions that were not "start-your-own-business" or commission-based types of jobs.

Many of the jobs posted are in the technology realm, but positions also appear for salespeople, consultants, writers, designers, and more. Even specialized positions for various types of professionals are included.

Employers pay a fee to have their company reviewed and approved; after that they submit jobs at no costs. Potential employees pay a monthly fee to get access to the job postings.

Of course, the same online sources you may currently use to find employees who will work onsite, also have the potential to be used to hire remote workers, your potential applicant market, though, expands when the work can be done anywhere.

General recruitment sites also still exist. While declining in usage somewhat because of the benefits of sites such as LinkedIn, these recruitment sites still remain a good source of candidates. Some of the more popular sites include Indeed.com, Monster.com, NationJob.com, and CareerBuilder.com. There are hundreds of others.

While large job boards such as Monster.com appeal to the masses, there are a number of industry-specific sites that can help you narrow your search. Sites such as Showbizjobs.com and Salesengineer.com provide both employers and job seekers with the ability to target their searches.

Obviously, not all of the online job seekers are looking for remote, or work-from-home opportunities. Still, the internet has been a definite boost both for those looking for remote work and for the employers who are looking for them.

The best way to become familiar with the recruiting resources available on the internet is to review the various services yourself, keeping in mind that you want to find one that is most advantageous for you. Smaller, more specialized services may be appropriate for your needs, depending on the type of position you are attempting to fill. Just as when you are recruiting through more traditional means, using a combination of resources can be the best way to promote your remote job openings.

5. Social Media and Recruitment

Social media and social networking are all the rage these days, of course. But, beyond the purely social aspects of sites such as Twitter, Facebook, and LinkedIn, does social media represent any legitimate business value? In the area of recruitment, it seems, it definitely does.

LinkedIn, for instance, is a great place for companies to find employees of any kind. Often used to find "passive" candidates, people with jobs currently that may have the skills you're looking for, LinkedIn offers the ability to search for potential candidates based on a wide range of criteria. One important point to note here, though, is that those who show up in a search will be dependent on your own network. Your search results will only display individuals who are your first- or second-degree connections, or who belong to the same groups that you do. For these reasons it's important for recruiters, business owners, HR professionals, and others to build a strong network to help boost the odds of finding top candidates.

Other social media channels may also offer opportunity to find remote workers. Facebook, for example, has a large number of groups, some that cater specifically to individuals looking for various types of jobs. For instance, The Copywriting Job Hub group is frequented by writers of various types focusing on a wide range of topic areas. This and other job-related groups can be a great place to post information about open positions and how to apply.

As far back as November 2006, National Public Radio had a spot on its "morning edition" about social networking, and its benefits from a recruiting standpoint. Today, these sites are becoming increasingly relied on by HR departments as a source of job candidates.

Jobvite (www.jobvite.com), a San Francisco-based provider of next-generation recruitment solutions, recently published the results of its tenth annual report, the 2020 Job Seeker Nation Report.

Its findings offer some important insights into how job seekers are learning about opportunities in the digital age:

- Online job boards (69%)

- Friends (45%)

- Social media sites such as LinkedIn (42%)

- Professional connections (31%)

In addition, according to its research, 68% of job seekers say remote work is "very" or "somewhat important" in making decisions about whether to accept a job offer. That's most likely to be the case among those with children at home (38%), with a college degree (33%), or men (32%).

Because of the "low cost of entry," there are no out-of-pocket costs associated with social media recruitment efforts. Time is money, of course. Some of the "fear" surrounding the use of social media is the time that may be required or diverted to learn about and "play with" these tools. Consequently, those considering this option should develop a strategy for their activities to avoid being overcome by the overwhelming amount of information and options available through these sites.

Even if you're not currently recruiting or not currently sure that social media holds value for you in terms of recruitment, it doesn't hurt to dabble in the social media environment.

Social media can be used in three primary ways when recruiting:

1. Posting available jobs

2. "Trolling" for potential candidates

3. "Checking out" applicants/interviewees

The internet makes it easy to find information about applicants to augment the traditional reference-checking process. Sites such as LinkedIn provide an opportunity to see what others may have said about the candidate in "recommendations."

6. Other Sources of Applicants

The digital environment isn't the only source of job applicants when searching for remote workers, of course. The traditional media may work well, depending on your specific needs. Placing classified ads in local newspapers or running ads in related trade journals still can be effective ways of reaching potential telecommuting candidates in the 21st century for certain types of positions.

Other sources of applicants include:

- **Job fairs:** Job fairs continue to be a popular source of job candidates (although, these, like other formerly live events have gone virtual during the COVID-19 pandemic). Generally organized by industry, job fairs are similar to trade shows that provide employers with the opportunity to meet interested job seekers in a particular field. For instance, a community might sponsor a small-manufacturing job fair at which area manufacturers would be present to provide information on their companies and their personnel needs.

- **Recruitment open houses:** Holding an open house for your own company provides you with the opportunity to present your job openings exclusively to a group of interested job candidates.

- **Recommendations and referrals:** Referrals from your existing employees can be a great source of potential telecommuting candidates. These referrals can generally be trusted after all, the employee has a vested interest in seeing the referral work out.

Rather than relying on any one source for applicants, use a combination of means to generate interest. Whatever means you use, be sure to clearly outline your needs and expectations. The recruitment stage is the critical first step toward ensuring that your telecommuters will be capable and productive.

7. Effective Online Recruiting

If you're recruiting online, you need to have the same familiarity with these services as you would with any technical or professional journal in which you were advertising. Who are the users of the site? What are their characteristics? How frequently is the site accessed? How widely do they advertise? Is the profession for which you are recruiting well represented?

The use of keywords — the search words that online job seekers will enter to pull up your listing — is a critical and often overlooked skill. You need to tie the appropriate keywords to your ads and you need to probe to make sure that your ads are being properly coded. If you have posted ads and wonder why you are not receiving any inquiries, the coding process may be the culprit. Each search engine is different, and you need to take the time to learn how each one functions and what sort of patterns there are in putting the keywords together. You don't want to code too restrictively or too broadly. Knowledge of how terminology is used in the field from which you're recruiting is a must.

A good way to become familiar with the technology is to practice with your own résumé or advertisement. This will give insight into how easy or difficult it is to access the online résumés of qualified candidates, or how easy it is for candidates to find your ad. If you post your résumé or ad to a service and it is not pulled up when you enter the keywords that you feel are most relevant, something is wrong.

There are literally thousands of individuals searching online job sites for positions. While a very general posting may provide you with countless leads, the more specific you can be, the more clearly you can narrow the market to only those candidates who are uniquely qualified to fill the positions you have available.

One of the potential downfalls of casting a wider net through online recruitment may be that your employer brand is not as widely known as it might be through other, more traditional, channels. Consequently, it can be harder to get the attention of the employees you're hoping to attract. Your employer brand works in very much the same way as your company, product, or service brand. In fact, your own existing and even past employees can serve as great employer brand ambassadors to help you spread the word about open positions, and to support the company as a great place to work.

You also must obviously be a great place to work. Sites such as Glassdoor.com have become very popular among employees as a way to share information about the companies they work, or worked, for — both good and bad — and as a tool for researching companies when they're looking for jobs. If you're not currently monitoring your own company on Glassdoor, you should be. And you should be responding to any negative comments you may see, correcting misinformation, or offering additional perspective or context.

8. Selection Criteria

On what evidence will you base your hiring decision? There are three commonly used selection measures for evaluating job applicants, including self-report, direct observation, and work samples. You may decide to use one or a combination of all three.

Self-report is the most commonly used measure. You ask the applicants about their accomplishments and experience, and they provide you with information that is, by its very nature, subject to bias. Direct observation, although often not possible, allows you to actually observe the candidates doing the work you will require. To approximate this measure, you might consider —

- using one of many tests that have been developed to measure various skills and abilities,

- role-playing certain tasks (i.e., sales calls, telemarketing scripts, etc.), or

- using hypothetical questions or situations to approximate real-life situations.

Work samples are appropriate for a number of positions that might lend themselves to telecommuting (i.e., computer programmers, website developers, writers, graphic designers).

The job specifications that you used to begin your employee search will play a major role in helping you make a final decision. Applicants should be evaluated both in terms of how well they meet the job specifications and how they compare to other applicants. For this reason, it is important to reserve a final decision until all interviews have been completed. Don't make a decision after each interview. It is best to wait until all interviews are completed and then rate interviewees on the basis of the criteria you have determined are the best predictors of job performance.

The selection process is subjective, leaving many areas open to bias and error. If you are aware of the possibility for error, you have taken one of the first steps to becoming a fair evaluator of job applicants. The following points can help make this demanding task a little less intimidating:

- Be prepared.

- Identify desired behaviors in observable rather than subjective terms.

- Be aware of your own personal biases and work to overcome them.

- Try using more than one interviewer and comparing results to determine possible bias.

- Don't assume that excellence in one area implies excellence in all areas.

- Base judgments on demonstrated performance, not anticipated performance.

Greg Hanover, CEO at Liveops says: "The first thing we look for when hiring remote workers is early signs of engagement. When working remotely, there is an additional degree of communication and engagement required to be successful. Be wary of a candidate who lacks enthusiasm at this stage, or appears distant from the process," Hanover cautions. "Ask yourself: Does this person seem fully engaged? Are they catching on quickly? You can be more confident that a remote style of work will not hinder a candidate's productivity or positive results in the role if their communication and transparency are already at the level required for remote success from the beginning."

Hanover also recommends assessing candidates' use of relevant technology during the interview process. "Remote employees need to be comfortable with video calls and virtual communication in general." For Liveops, says Hanover, that means asking candidates about their proficiency levels with breakout rooms, voting, and chat functionalities all applications the company requires employees to use.

When hiring remote workers, it's important to ask the right questions, says Hanover. "While it's good to know about a candidate's history and experience, the success of a remote employee relies heavily on specific behavioral qualities," he says. For example:

- Tell me about a time when you managed a team in a remote environment?

- How do you stay connected?

- In what ways do you stay visible while working remotely?

- How do you stay motivated without an office environment?

Once you get answers to your basic questions, Hanover recommends moving into a conversation about what works best for the candidates in terms of working remotely. "Ask them to share their best practices," he says. "Have a conversation where they share a description of their best remote boss and what specific qualities of that relationship made them worthy of that title," he suggests.

Another important area of exploration, says Hanover, is work/life balance. "It is critical that your employees can create a line between their work and their time off when both largely occur in the same space. Make sure that your candidates have a home office that enables them to be productive, successful and professional."

In addition to the selection criteria mentioned above, employers will also want to seek references from former employers when hiring remote staff, in the same manner they would when hiring onsite staff. These references will, of course, be particularly useful if the employee previously worked from a remote setting.

The goal when hiring remote employees, says Hanover, is to "obtain a holistic view of their style of work. With this information you'll be able to more clearly decide whether a role is right for the candidate or not."

9. Interviewing Candidates for Off-site Jobs

Interviewing candidates for remote work can be done far more conveniently and creatively than one might imagine. For example, your first interview might actually take place online, via email. After all, if this is the means by which you will most frequently communicate with your telecommuting employees, doesn't it make sense to get a good idea of their skills in this medium up front? From there, you may want to go on to a telephone interview. Eventually, but not always, you may want to bring the candidates into your office.

The interview process will be much the same as the process for hiring any employee. Focus on the criteria you've established for the position and develop questions designed to determine if the candidates have the experience, background, and personal traits and characteristics that will enable them to be successful telecommuters.

Your goal is to identify behaviors that will lead to successful job performance and to devise questions that let you determine if applicants will be a good fit. Project yourself into the future. Look back and describe the ideal outcome. This gives you a sense of what a good person to hire "looks like."

When you ask questions of your telecommuting candidates, you want to gather as much information as possible and probe for meaningful responses. Your interviewing skills will determine whether or not you gather all the pertinent information. While there are never any guarantees that the person you hire will work out, a well-conducted interview will improve your chances of making an informed decision.

When interviewing employees remotely via video conferencing technology, in particular, there are some important issues to be aware of. Chief among these are privacy and security, access to technology, and the impacts of artificial intelligence (AI) in evaluating candidates.

Privacy and security issues should always be top of mind, but remote hiring practices raise different issues. Zoom, for instance, was in the media at the beginning of 2020 because of various hacks of its system that resulted in unauthorized individuals joining meetings. To keep this from happening users are cautioned to both require a password to enter the meeting and to "wait in a waiting room" until the meeting organizer can approve their admission.

Another privacy issue relates to how employers may use, and how they must store, any videotaped interviews. Employers should indicate to potential employees not only who will be in the actual interview, but who may have access to the recording after the interview. In addition, recordings become part of the employment record and need to be retained in accordance with EEOC Uniform Guidelines on Employee Selection Procedures.

Access to technology can be another concern. Candidates may not have equal access. Some may have access to high-speed internet connections, others may not. Some may choose to participate in an interview from their desktop computer, others from their smartphones. These may yield different types of experiences for candidates and different types of impressions from interviewers.

If you will be using any form of AI technology in scoring interviews, candidates must be informed in certain states. For instance,

Illinois passed a new law in 2020 that requires employers to disclose to candidates if AI scoring will be done, other states are expected to follow.

Finally, make sure that anyone involved in the video interviewing process has been trained and is prepared to participate in what could be a very different type of experience.

10. References

According to HireRight's 2019 Employment Screening Benchmark Report, more than 20% of candidates misrepresent their experience or background up from 10% in 2018.

Most hiring mistakes can be prevented through proper reference-checking procedures. Unfortunately, countless employers neglect this important step in the hiring process. They rely instead on their own impressions of the candidate based on the résumé, application, and interview. This is a major mistake and it can be costly. Checking the references of your telecommuting applicants is essential to obtain accurate information about qualifications and experience.

Many employers call references after interviews have been conducted. Making these calls beforehand can help you filter out undesirable candidates earlier, saving time that you would have spent in an interview. Checking references before the interview can also provide you with additional areas to explore during the interview, and can help you formulate pertinent questions in advance.

Before checking references, prepare questions and have a clear idea of the information you hope to obtain. You will want to ask questions related to the applicant's ability to work independently, to be productive, and to achieve results. Keep in mind that some organizations have policies against giving a great deal of information about former or current employees and will provide little detail beyond length of service and rate of pay. Still, it pays to be persistent and to ask for additional sources of information along the way. Try asking, "Is there anyone else I should speak with?"

Try these questions when checking references for potential remote employees:

- What type of remote work did the candidate do with your firm?

- How often did the candidate work remotely?

- How much direction did the applicant need?

- Did the applicant consistently meet deadlines?

- How were the applicant's problem-solving skills?

- Tell me about the applicant's communication skills.

- In your opinion, is this a person who can work well in a remote position with minimal supervision?

11. Perils and Pitfalls

Any hiring decision is important, but when hiring remote workers, you must be particularly vigilant. Because you will be relying on them to be self-sufficient and reliable, you need to make sure that you take the time to clearly identify the type of candidate you need, to interview carefully, to check references, and to make hiring decisions based on objective criteria. There are a number of potential perils and pitfalls that you should be aware of as you go through this process:

- **Not adapting your processes and procedures to the online environment:** The world is changing, technology is changing, and your hiring practices need to change too. Many of the steps you have taken in the past will not convert readily or efficiently to online venues. Be flexible and willing to adapt whenever necessary.

- **Limiting yourself to one or two sources of applicants:** Don't give up on traditional sources of recruiting, such as newspapers or trade journals. Take advantage of the plethora of recruitment sites, and keep up with new additions. Be adventurous and be constantly alert to new online opportunities.

- **Overlooking local or regional sites:** Local communities frequently have job-site listings at chamber of commerce or local newspaper sites. If you're located in Minnesota, but want to tap into the technological expertise you believe exists in San Francisco, check out some of the local San Francisco sites in addition to the major national sites.

- **Not using the sites yourself:** The best way to learn about recruitment over the internet is to actively visit and use the various sites. As a user you can test the search capabilities, posting opportunities, content, and general usability of these sites.

- **Comparing apples to oranges:** One of the benefits and downfalls of the internet is that even the least experienced and least reputable organizations can develop sites that present a "Wow!" image. Don't be too easily taken in by the glamorous front. Carefully consider the types of postings the site offers, the number of postings, and the charges (direct and hidden) before making any decision to pay for services.

Just as you need a system for creating policies and procedures for those situations where employees are working in a nontraditional location, you also need a systematic approach to considering individual candidates. How structured your selection criteria are will depend on your company's culture as well as on your comfort level with the concept of managing off-site staff. Even companies that have been committed to these flexible arrangements for some time often have very stringent criteria for selecting candidates.

Alison Bernstein, founder and president of Suburban Jungle, says: "Remote workers need to be self-starters. When hiring it must be crystal clear to me from the onset that this is someone who can take the initiative. This is key. For those that sit and wait for direction, this is not the right gig. It is first and foremost for those that have a higher level of executive functioning and can organize their days to make the most of them. It isn't just about being results-driven, it is about simply being driven."

12. Lessons from the Trenches

Melissa Smith is a remote work consultant and the founder and CEO of the Association of Virtual Assistants and The PVA. While no site will ever take the place of your own network and "constantly cultivating relationships," Smith says that when she's conducting private searches she uses private communities where experienced remote workers already are, for instance, Remotive.io and LinkedIn.

When hiring, she says, she places a focus on "the three C's — communication strategy, company mission, and culture fit." All companies are not the same and neither are all remote companies. They are, she says, "as diverse as brick and mortar companies." "The idea that working for a remote company is the equivalent of working for a Google or Facebook-like company is not realistic. Freedom, flexibility, and autonomy cannot be assumed," she says.

As when hiring for any position, companies are looking for a good fit. "A solid hiring process looks at the big picture and understands the need to hire in the same way the company runs on a daily basis," says Smith. "There should be an entire plan of action written. Making it up as you go along is a very costly mistake." In addition, she says, it's important to explain to candidates what they can expect from the hiring process, why you're using the process you're using and how they can be most successful during the process.

Some questions that Smith feels are critical to making a good choice when hiring remote staff are questions related to how the candidates communicate, how they ask for help, and the practices they use for self-care and setting boundaries. "If the candidate is not communicative or doesn't prefer to communicate in the methods that the company does, it will never work," she warns. "Not everyone is comfortable asking for help and, in an office, this can be done casually. Remotely it is done deliberately." In remote work settings, she stresses, employers don't have the opportunity to "see someone and know how they are feeling." It's important, therefore, to ensure that employees will be proactive and that they will feel comfortable seeking help, both for work-related issues and for issues related to their well-being.

Chapter 7

ONBOARDING

Onboarding is a natural step in welcoming new employees to the workplace. It's an opportunity to introduce employees to company policies and procedures, places, and personnel. The first few days and weeks on the job are critical; even more so when the employee will be working remotely.

During the pandemic, employers were faced with some new scenarios for onboarding. They needed to onboard employees who had never previously worked physically with the organization and, because of the virus, would begin their days with the organization working remotely; onboarding, or re-onboarding, employees who had been deployed to remote locations but were being brought back to work onsite, or onboarding new employees who would be physically working at the organization.

In each of these situations the processes and information needed to be conveyed are similar, but there are some variations that are important for employers to consider.

1. The New World of Onboarding during COVID-19

From a COVID-19 standpoint, says Andrea Zoia, with Morgan, Brown & Joy, an employment law firm in Boston, "as employers are starting to return employees to the 'new normal' in the workplace, they should take the opportunity to explain to their workers what has changed and what has not and anticipate the concerns employees are likely to have upon their return." There will be state and local regulations and requirements to be aware of, she says, but "at minimum, this explanation should include any changes related to employees' salary and benefits and work expectations as well as how the employer is proactively taking steps to ensure workplace safety, and the worker's role in that endeavor."

In addition to complying with any required notification and training requirements applicable to them, says Zoia, employers should ensure that their workplace safety rules are communicated clearly and in a manner most effective to their workplace.

"Ideally, rules will be communicated in advance in writing electronically and posted at workstations and common areas," she says. "All training materials and related postings should be easy to understand and in appropriate language for all employees; the more accessible the new rules are, the more likely they will be followed."

Some workforces will benefit from video or remote training prior to returning to work to introduce them to the new workplace rules, says Zoia and, of course, for those employees being hired to work remotely, this will be the best way to provide them with critical information about the company and their new role. In addition to the training received by the rest of the employees, Zoia says, "employers should not overlook providing employees with managerial responsibility additional training and guidance on how to enforce social distancing rules and other required practices."

But, despite the pandemic or its continued presence, it will continue to be important for remote workers to be onboarded just as onsite workers are in fact, arguably more important. Recognizing the importance of starting employees off with the knowledge and information they need to be successful, some employers are even beginning the onboarding process before an employee actually begins their official role, a practice known as "pre-boarding."

1.1 Preboarding – setting the stage for future success

According to one expert, first impressions of your organization begin before a new hire comes on board, which means it's time to rethink your onboarding process.

Erwin van der Vlist, Founder and CEO of Speakap, refers to pre-boarding as "the new onboarding." "It's an effort geared primarily toward the Millennial and Gen Z populations," he says.

With millennials dominating today's workplaces, it's important for organizations to connect with them in meaningful ways. For millennials, that means "fostering a sense of purpose and fulfillment early on through platforms they find familiar," Van Der Vlist says. He offers four strategies for doing that:

1. Begin Relevant Engagement Immediately. Waiting until employees' first days on the job is too long. They're likely giving a lot of thought to the important decision they just made to join your company, perhaps even having second thoughts. Reaching out to them to support the smart decision they just made, and demonstrate the value they will find working with the company and their new team members, can help engage them before they're formally on the payroll.

2. Tap into Their Need for Connection with Digital Communications Tools. The youngest members of your workforce grew up with technology and are very comfortable with it. Their smartphones are with them almost 24/7 and are the prime vehicles they use to get messages from friends and family and stay up to date on news and events. Employers need to keep this in mind and make sure they move beyond traditional email communications to offer other digital channels and platforms Millennials and Gen Z feel most comfortable with.

3. Encourage Sharing to Forge Early Relationships. "Digital channels can ease new employees into the work community," Van Der Vlist says. He encourages companies to make online and social introductions through these channels as a precursor to the actual introductions that will come later. This also provides an opportunity to introduce new employees to whatever enterprise social networks the company uses and gives them the opportunity to explore them a bit before starting the new job.

4. Integrate Company Tools and Training to Ease the Transition. As digital channels, apps, and tools proliferate in the workplace, all of the sign-ons, passwords, and processes can become a bit overwhelming, especially in light of everything else a new employee needs to learn. A single sign-on can simplify this process, creating more efficiency for all.

Steps taken to make new employees, especially new remote employees, feel welcome before they even join the organization can be a great way to build engagement at the outset and ensure these remote employees feel welcome and included.

2. Social Considerations

One critical element to ensure that new employees will quickly feel that they're part of the team is opportunities for interaction outside the scope of work assignments — social connections that can help new team members get to know their colleagues, both those who are also remote and those who may be physically in the workplace.

Well-managed company social events can provide a boost to employee training and onboarding in a number of ways. For instance:

- **Creating opportunities for networking:** One of the major benefits and purposes of company gatherings is to serve as a means of internal networking. Employees can get to know key resources from throughout the organization and develop relationships that bolster collaborative work. This is particularly true for new employees who are often at a loss when trying to identify key staff members who might be able to provide input, resources, or a source of escalation for work the new employee is engaged in.

- **Providing a forum for informal conversation:** Company-sponsored social events provide an opportunity for staff to have discussions outside of formal meetings. Employees may struggle with various aspects of their work, new processes, or unfamiliar industry knowledge. The opportunity for informal interactions with others can open the door to important connections. Discussions with seasoned staff and even fellow trainees and new recruits can help bring greater understanding to the nuances of what they've been learning. For companies with remote staff, these gatherings can occur either virtually or in person. Both can be valued ways of making connections.

- **Cultural socialization:** Company get-togethers help immerse new staff members in the company culture. They get more exposure to how employees interact with coworkers, superiors, and subordinates; they also get a flavor for the current key areas of importance and relevance within the company based on conversations with other staff.

The social aspects of onboarding are important for both onsite and off-site staff, but are often not given as much attention as they should be. Off-site staff, in particular, need to have opportunities to make and build connections with colleagues and, in some case, customers and vendors. This should be considered a critical part of the onboarding process.

What opportunities do you have, or might you create, to help your newly hired remote staff quickly feel like they're a valued part of the organization and that they have had opportunities to get to know their colleagues?

3. Additional Implications for Remote Workers

Andrew Meadows is senior vice president at Ubiquity Retirement + Savings, in San Francisco, a company that employs 85 people, 85% of them working from home.

While many companies likely stress employee training, Meadows said he believes the week new hires spend in orientation is a "big deal to us. It's the most important part of employee life because it's rigorous and sets the stage for success with the company."

Employees fly to San Francisco for a week to learn of the client life cycle, take aptitude and skills assessments, and hear briefings from every department before joining their boss to learn the actual job. In addition, they spend time learning about the technology they will use from home. ScreenSteps, an integrated knowledge base that Meadows calls a "living" user manual will guide them through process and procedure questions, and they learn how success is measured.

Initially, says Morgan Taylor, CMO for LetMeBank, onboarding remote staff is going to seem challenging. But, he says: "Once you've got your onboarding videos and techniques mastered, you'll realize that it's actually easier. Instead of going over everything individually, again and again, you drop them the link to the prerecorded Zoom video, hit them up on a live meeting afterwards for a brief group Q&S, and you're done."

Greg Hanover, CEO of Liveops stresses the importance of acclimating employees to the culture of the organization quickly, "while it may be more difficult to cultivate in a remote environment, it still holds the same, if not a greater, importance," he says. "I've found that taking time to foster inclusion and a team atmosphere in a remote environment can make or break an organization."

When onboarding, Hanover says, make sure new employees understand that they're part of the team. "It is crucial that you express your expectations with as much clarity as possible and that new team members know who they can go to for help when needed. Prioritize openness and transparency through consistent and frequent communication. Discuss your core beliefs, how to live them, and how your employees can measure themselves against them."

It's also important for remote employees to have the opportunity to meet their colleagues, even if they won't be physically working together. "Communication is critical, and in a remote environment it needs to be done by design and not by default," Hanover says. "Having a structure in place to foster an inclusive, remote environment requires work, planning, and time. You have to be intentional about bringing the 'water cooler talk' online, whether that be through Slack channels to show off your kids, pets, or kudos for great work, monthly mixers and virtual happy hours, or small group conversations that allow you to take a break from work-mode."

Employees won't have the opportunity to "meet" their colleagues or customers if you don't set aside the time for them to do so. Incorporating a planned strategy with regularly delivered messages will improve employees' onboarding experiences.

4. Lessons from the Trenches

Ashley Sterling is director of operations at The Loop Marketing, a digital marketing agency based in Chicago, who found herself suddenly working from home during the pandemic. The biggest adjustment, she says, "has been the challenge to create a consistent schedule with personal and work life." It's easy, she says, to "fall into the, I'll just answer a few emails' rhythm and before you know it you've worked 50+ hours or more. Establishing, and sticking to, a schedule is vital, she says.

Prior to COVID-19, she says, the company had the ability to work remotely so the transition may have bene easier than for other companies without that option previously. For The Loop, she says, "the easy access to all of our resources in the event of a last-minute project, or an urgent matter, makes our customer service capabilities remain consistent."

For her personally, though, social interaction is something she misses. She says she is "definitely missing seeing people on a day-to-day basis and having the luxury of communicating in person." She's also missing the routine of heading into the office which helps to keep her focused.

It's important, she says, for people to create an at-home work environment that works for them. "No two people are the same, do you need complete silence? Do you need a window? Do you need music? Do you need the TV on? Adjust your hours? There is no wrong answer. Make your space your space as much as possible."

After the pandemic she predicts that The Loop will continue to offer at-home work options, potentially to a greater degree than it had in the past. But, she says, after this experience, "We all recognize the importance of meeting face-to-face to ensure proper communication."

Chapter 8

TRAINING OFF-SITE AND ONSITE WORKERS, MANAGERS, AND SUPERVISORS

As we've already discussed, remote workers are not the only off-site staff that could benefit from training related to how they can be most effective and productive in remote locations. Whether working from a home office, a branch office, or on an international assignment, the ability to communicate effectively, and use the tools that the organization has available to expedite work processes, is critical.

To be most effective, training should be considered, from the very beginning, as a program or process that allows workers to work from locations other than the main office.

Emily Goodson is founder and CEO of CultureSmart, a consulting firm based in San Diego, that works with startups of less than 100 employees. In the past, says Goodson, many companies have doled out work-from-home opportunities as privileges for high performers. Not anymore. Because of COVID-19, it's now become an imperative that companies need to recognize and prepare their employees, particularly managers, with specific training, she says.

"As a country, we're grappling with the fact that our workplaces will never look the same," Goodson says. "We certainly won't go back to the office in full capacity and because of health and risk factors, it may not be feasible. Some employees won't go back to the office at all; others like working from home and don't want to lose the opportunity."

Giving WFM flexibility across the board "means that managers will need to manage all types of employees, not just the high performers," Goodson says. To ensure that managers are successful, they need training.

1. Characteristics of Employee Training Programs

Employee training programs generally have the following characteristics:

- Individual sessions are conducted for employees and their managers; both groups are brought together at some point to participate in planning and general discussion.

- Technology is an element of training, but it takes a backseat to more critical issues such as a heavy emphasis on communication skills, establishment of measurable goals, and discussion of how to measure progress.

- A focus on some of the "softer" issues such as how to deal with interruptions at home and how to handle isolation, and a sharing of experiences are important parts of the training process.

Companies that have been working with off-site employees for some time have incorporated training into the process, recognizing its importance. In many of these companies, training is broken down into three parts: training for employees; training for supervisors/managers; and "team training" — that is, outlining opportunities for the employees and their manager to come together and discuss the issues that impact the relationship.

This three-tiered training structure is an essential tool for implementing and maintaining relationships that work. Let's have a closer look at how these three facets of training operate.

Alexis Haselberger is a productivity, time management, and leadership coach based in San Francisco. "Because the in-person classroom model doesn't work for remote workers, we have to figure out how to make Zoom classes engaging and interactive, so people aren't just staring at a screen for hours," she says. "In my virtual workshops I do this in a number of ways. Each participant receives a fillable PDF workbook that allows us to do exercises during the workshop," she says. "We use breakout rooms and polling for interaction. For smaller groups, 20 or less, we can allow people to unmute, ask questions, and engage. For larger groups we can use chat to ask and answer questions."

Successful off-site work relationships don't just happen because an employee who used to work in the office now works from home. It's not quite that simple. There are certain differences between working at the head office and working at home. Those differences need to be covered through training and orientation to ensure that the employee knows what to expect and is capable of making the transition.

2. Managers Need Training Too

Your efforts to allow for alternative work arrangements will fall apart very quickly if you train only the employees and not their managers. You will not only have to be concerned with implementing a revised management structure and approach for people who manage remote staff.

Your first challenge will be to overcome the prevailing attitudes and fears that your managers may have toward employees who are "out of sight."

The resistance of supervisors and managers is a common barrier to implementing alternative work arrangements, and one that must be tackled head-on at an early stage in the process.

This is unfamiliar territory for many supervisors and managers and, as human beings, we tend to raise barriers when faced with the unknown or any form of change that we are ill-prepared for. In fact, the typical "if I can't see them, how do I know if they're really working" concern is often a smokescreen masking other concerns that managers may have. Learning to make the transition from managing time to managing projects is a critical shift for many managers.

Gil Gordon who was an early proponent of remote work and who has coached and counseled numerous off-site staff, managers, and others about best practices related to remote work said: "I think managers often believe that they know more about managing and are more competent at it than they really are." In fact, this belief isn't just related to managing off-site staff, but managing staff in general. Many managers have not received formal training in managing others, they were promoted into management roles because of their expertise as individual contributors.

Gordon's approach to training managers "is mostly a matter of fine-tuning what we hope they're already doing and maybe introducing some new concepts, as opposed to starting from scratch, which is not necessary and which will not gain many fans," he says.

The message is: Keep it simple. You don't need to create chaos among your managers. You simply need to look at the employee-manager relationship and address the basic issues. Even training on such simple skills as how to communicate effectively via phone, email, and video conferencing solutions can have a positive effect on the manager/employee relationship.

Communication, foundationally, is the key to effective management of off-site staff and this should be a major focus of any training initiative. Managers need to be sensitive to maintaining a high level of communication with off-site staff, keeping them involved and recognizing that managing someone you don't physically see or interact with on a regular basis is considerably different than running into them in the breakroom or speaking across a table in a meeting.

When Gordon regularly conducted training sessions for managers, he offered a two-hour session designed to improve managerial relationships with remote staff by "taking the guesswork out of remote work and making sure that everyone has thought through the critical issues." The following topics were generally covered:

- Managing by results instead of by observation
- Fine-tuning skills for setting performance standards and giving ongoing performance feedback
- Keeping remote workers tied to the office or physical workspace
- Career management issues
- Spotting problems early and dealing with them effectively

As part of the process it can also be helpful to offer some specific information on expectations for the management process, or helpful tips that can aid managers in effectively overseeing their staff, whether onsite or off-site because this is generally not an "all or nothing" situation. Managers are likely to be responsible for a mixture of people who may be working from home, or other locations, or may be onsite. Managers themselves may be either onsite or off-site, which was especially true during stay-at-home orders during the coronavirus pandemic.

3. Training Onsite Employees

In addition to off-site employees and their supervisors and managers, onsite employees should receive training and communication about how to work effectively with their off-site colleagues. The workforce at large also needs to have some training and education to familiarize them with the alternative work arrangements that are part of the company's operations.

"Employees will need to advocate for themselves and what they need," says Haselberger. "All circumstances are different and, if your manager is not in the same room with you, it might be harder to tell if you are struggling," she says. "We'll need to have more proactive conversations with employees about training needs."

For those with both onsite and off-site staff, a team approach to training can be especially effective, providing an opportunity for interaction and the ability to bring up questions and issues —and discuss them on the spot.

Managers can discuss what they expect from employees and the type of communication they will use. They can discuss in real-time how the relationships and interactions between employees will work.

In Gordon's experiences with training, he says: "The joint sessions I find the most interesting and attendees do too. It's really a negotiating and planning session." At these sessions employees and managers can discuss such issues as:

- How many days a week employees will be working off-site, which days will they be, how often should they check in? As mundane as these questions may seem, according to Gordon,

"I have seen over and over again that if they are not discussed in advance, you wind up with two very different sets of expectations that are really pretty dangerous when they come up against each other." Consequently, team sessions could include a focus on the following:

- Detailing the schedule, available, phone coverage, and office days

- Planning the first few weeks of interacting with off-site staff

- Minimizing the effects of off-site work on department workflow and productivity

- Providing technical (equipment) support as needed

- Dealing with system shutdowns and other problems

The workforce at large also needs to have some training and education to familiarize them with the alternative work arrangements that are part of the company's operations. If the entire workforce isn't trained and educated about existing alternative options and how they impact the work of the department, division or company, both productivity and engagement can be impacted.

4. Lessons from the Trenches

Emily Goodson is founder and CEO of CultureSmart, a consulting firm based in San Diego, that works with startups of fewer than 100 employees. In the past, says Goodson, many companies have doled out work-from-home opportunities as privileges for high performers. Not anymore. Because of COVID-19, it's now become imperative that companies recognize and prepare employees, particularly managers, with specific training.

"As a country, we're grappling with the fact that our workplaces will never look the same," Goodson says. "We certainly won't go back to the office in full capacity and because of health and risk factors, it may not be feasible. Some employees won't go back to the office at all, and others like working from home and don't want to lose the opportunity."

Giving WFM flexibility across the board "means that managers will need to manage all types of employees — not just the high performers," Goodson says.

To ensure that managers are successful, they need training that focuses on intentional communication and engagement, which is how we build connections and safety.

When speaking of safety, Goodson is referring to psychological safety. For example, it means that employees feel safe receiving and giving feedback; that they feel safe challenging the status quo; and they feel safe admitting that they made a mistake and now need help.

"Much has been written about psychological safety because of Wells Fargo," Goodson says, citing the banking firm as an example. If employees had felt safe speaking up about sales productivity measures that resulted in fraud, perhaps the company and its customers could have been spared the controversy, penalties, and damage to its brand.

That's an extreme example, but most people who have been working at home since the coronavirus was declared a pandemic in March likely can relate to naturally feeling more distant and disconnected while working. "When people feel like they are on an island, it's not as natural to seek help," Goodson says. "It's so much easier to knock on someone's office door to ask for help."

"Managers of remote teams can make all the difference with communication and engagement," she says. "They can relate to the team and calm down expectations by setting expectations to make sure it's not awkward to ask for help."

To ensure that managers understand intentional communication, Goodson said they should think about volume and channels.

"Sometimes managers struggle with remote teams because they can't see them. They can't see how they are working on their projects or if they are working on their projects. At times, they will use Instant Message almost every minute to ensure they have the employee's attention. That's distracting and it's conveying distrust," Goodson says .

To combat that, managers should communicate communication channels and the circumstances in which they will be used, such as that they expect the team will —

- pick up the phone for urgent or personal situations;
- use email for updates that are timely, but not urgent; and

- use instant messaging when they need a response within two hours, for example.

Goodson is hearing from people who indicate that they haven't had any one-on-one communication with their managers. "A quick check-in is easy when everyone is in the office," she says said. Now, managers need to be more intentional.

"I've heard some horror stories about managers who have not talked to their employees in over a month," she says. "From the top down, those expectations about regular communication need to be set."

"It would be good for executive management to say to managers: We know you aren't trained to manage a remote work force, but let me help.

"Without the intentional communication, it will be nearly impossible to manage performance and productivity issues," Goodson says. "If someone is underperforming, and you decide to let them go, HR isn't going to sign off on it if you haven't delivered documented feedback in a routine and intentional way.

"I'm hearing a lot, too, about parents who are struggling with caregiving and teaching while trying to work," she says. "This situation is going to continue during the summer as camps and other activities for children are canceled." Companies need to discuss any productivity issues especially in unprecedented times. Flexibility may be key. Perhaps some employees need the freedom to work different hours to help accommodate their children and other obligations.

Goodson pointed to emotional intelligence as an issue for remote teams. She said research by professor, author and lecturer Brene Brown's team found that people can usually identify only three emotions — bad, sad, and glad.

"If you can't name an emotion, it's hard to manage it," she says. "When you can name an emotion, you have more power over it, which will help you move on and cope.

"When you have a life, you bring all of it with you to the workspace," she explains.

In terms of advice for companies, she says, it's essential to survey your workforce about their preferences for working remotely. In particular, it's important to ask about the pain points and what the company could or should fix. Because of the uncertainty of bringing workers back to the office, Goodson thinks companies will continue offering flexibility in location and even in which executive positions could be based away from the corporate headquarters.

One trouble spot that Goodson pointed out is data security. Because a remote workforce can open a company's software, documents, and files to more people, there are more opportunities for data breaches and hacking. That needs to be addressed with audits and technology investments, she says.

Chapter 9

MANAGING OFF-SITE STAFF – BEST PRACTICES

In the vast majority of situations, employees who work in off-site locations come from within the organization and have held a position with the company for some time before making the transition. There are obvious benefits to selecting employees to work in off-site arrangements from your existing staff. You already know these people! You've had a chance to view their work habits and performance. You know which of your employees are independent and proactive and which employees need constant supervision and direction.

But there can be downfalls as well, particularly if you don't take the time to make informed and carefully considered choices about which employees are offered these opportunities. Even when assigning employees to branch locations or other affiliated sites where they won't have direct supervision, it is important to consider the traits and characteristics of these employees to ensure that they're right for this type of work.

Even when managers have direct line-of-sight contact with members of their staff, managing employees can be a challenge. Many managers become managers because of their expertise in their field, without having any formal management training. Frequently, they learn through trial and error. It's not surprising, then, that managers often balk at nontraditional work arrangements. Managing is hard enough without the added stress and uncertainty of trying to keep track of people who aren't even in the building! Managers are often reluctant or wary when it comes to the consideration of work arrangements in which employees are out of sight. Misconceptions abound, and these misconceptions can prevent alternative work arrangements from developing, or sabotage them once they're in place. But what managers sometimes don't realize is that allowing employees flexibility in their schedules and work locations can easily become a win-win situation, improving manager-employee relations, management techniques and effectiveness, and productivity.

1. The Truth about Managing Off-site Staff

While the many misconceptions associated with remote work can certainly keep companies from moving toward this flexible option, the biggest factor that limits the practice at many companies is trust. Managing remote workers can require a major paradigm shift for many organizations and individuals. Rather than believing that you are paying an employee for his or her time, you must move to an understanding that you are paying an employee for his or her output — whether that output is measured in number of sales, completion of specific projects, or consultation.

Managing remote workers doesn't really require different strengths and capabilities than managing in traditional environments. It does, however, require that managers have strong management skills.

Good managers are good managers — whether supervising employees who work in the same physical location they do, or supervising employees in remote locations. Basic management tools are just as important for remote staff as they are for people in the office, but you may need to tailor your supervision for those working at home. "Management by walking around" won't work.

You'll probably find that you need to focus more on results than appearance. Scheduling might get tricky. And you'll be called upon to show trust and support to employees who are working remotely, and to those who are not.

Results are what count, not face time, putting in long hours, working overtime, or any of the other traditional ways of measuring performance. This is much the same as any other type of management except it truly tests your skills. It requires an added level of communication, more carefully crafted and measurable objectives, and clear and direct feedback.

The traits of successful managers of off-site workers are actually no different from the traits of any successful managers, with the exception, perhaps, of a heightened need for excellence in setting goals and objectives, establishing job standards, communication, and providing feedback.

2. Set Goals and Objectives

Employee performance, whether employees are on- or off-site, should be measured on the attainment of established goals and objectives. Managers must set and articulate clear goals, making sure that both they and their employees understand what is expected. In addition, more frequent evaluation may be necessary where performance, goals, and expectations can be discussed along with a thorough evaluation of any signs of problems or emerging issues.

Loren Howard is the owner of Prime Plus Mortgages and other entities; based in Paradise Valley, Arizona. For nearly 15 years, Loren Howard has mainly used remote employees and has worked virtually himself. In fact, his small group of employees represent a variety of countries, including India, the Philippines, and the United States. When the pandemic hit, Howard used some of the down time to upgrade systems. He cited the wisdom of anglers, who say, "when the seas won't allow you to fish, you tend to the nets." Howard offers the following tips for helping to establish, and align, employees around goals to drive company performance:

- Use a management system to help with your annual and quarterly planning. The type or name brand doesn't matter as long as you use the system consistently for strategic planning, workflow, management tracking, KPIs, etc.

- Be sure your entire workforce "remote or in-office" understands the value of a management system and reinforce habits for its long-term use.

- Conduct an annual planning session using facilitators, again ensuring that all employees understand the value of planning and setting objectives.

- Create or purchase a system for tracking productivity, and "let the system be the bad guy when it comes to discipline or letting someone go." Howard explained that the system can be your checks and balances. Is the employee accountable or not? Is work getting done to the required metric and specification or not? The conversations are easier to have when using data.

Well-defined goals allow both the telecommuter and manager to have a clear understanding of expectations and provide a benchmark against which to judge performance.

Goals should be:

- Specific. A goal should state "Increase sales by 20 percent," rather than simply "Increase sales."

- Mutually agreed upon.

- Difficult, yet achievable.

- Comprehensive. Goals should cover all critical areas of the telecommuter's job.

Establishing the details of goals and objectives should be the joint responsibility of the manager and his or her employees. Together, they should cover the following tasks:

- Identify objectives based on organizational and departmental goals. If a system of measurement is already in place, it should work just as well in a remote working relationship as it does in the office.

- Develop schedules with assigned responsibility for specific task completion. Make it very clear who will be responsible for what and when deliverables are expected. Be sure that employees know how their performance is being measured and what the standards for performance are.

- Set up times to determine the progress of the employees' tasks. This may be a designated point during the program, upon completion of certain tasks, or on a recurring (e.g., weekly) basis.

- Establish ongoing means of communicating work expectations, including due dates, quality expectations, and any other measurable criteria. This may include face-to-face meetings, electronic submission of reports, or conference calls.

It is important that the manager take the time to become familiar with the employees' work responsibilities and tasks.

Managers must understand the time involved for completing tasks and the resources required to see projects through to completion. They must ensure that goals for off-site staff are neither more nor less stringent than those set for employees doing similar work at the office. They must establish a smoothly functioning working relationship with off-site employees, and above all, they must communicate every last detail, in detail.

Some of these details will inevitably have to be worked out along the way, as individual employees, with their specific needs and situations, settle into a work routine. However, some basic considerations can be dealt with from the start. Managers should consider the following:

- Are there core hours during which you want employees to be available?

- Are work hours flexible?

- How often should employees call the office or check their voice mail and email?

- How quickly should employees return messages?

- How often should employees communicate with their clients and coworkers?

- What security or confidentiality issues may be involved?

One of the most important things that managers can do, not just when managing off-site staff, but when managing any staff is to be very clear about the expectations they have for the employee. Taking the time to lay out these expectations at the outset of the relationship can help to avoid potential issues later and can boost the odds of a successful experience for everyone.

3. Establish Job Standards

How will an employee's work be evaluated? What level of productivity will be expected? What are the criteria by which the employee's work output will be judged? Be specific. By clearly outlining expectations at the outset, you can avoid misunderstandings and frustration later.

Establishing job standards is a process that begins the moment an employee — onsite or remote — is hired and continues throughout the employment relationship. It involves clear communication of expectations and the development of specific, measurable goals, which we have already discussed.

The job description is a good starting point for indicating what is expected, but it is just a starting point. An explanation of job standards can help indicate to employees the specific expectations for a position.

Employees also need to know the goals of their positions and how those goals tie into department and company performance.

The first step in developing job standards is to identify the critical aspects of the job. What elements of the position are necessary to keep the department and the company operating efficiently? Once the areas of responsibility have been identified, three or four standards (or key results) that represent satisfactory performance levels need to be established. It is critical that these standards be objective measures of performance. More specifically, managers can use the following measures in establishing standards:

- **Quality:** How many errors, omissions, or complaints will you tolerate over a given period of time?

- **Quantity:** How many units of production will you expect over a given period of time?

- **Timeliness:** Time standards can be written in terms of daily, weekly, monthly, or quarterly deadlines for task completion or amount of turnaround time permitted.

- **Cost efficiency:** Some positions have responsibility for meeting budgets or impacting costs. In these cases your standards might reflect a maximum dollar budget or a plus or minus variance from the stated budget.

Unfortunately, not all job tasks readily lend themselves to establishing clearly defined standards. It can be challenging to come up with quantifiable measurements for certain tasks. Your goal should be to define the most critical elements of the job and, at a minimum, to establish standards that are clear enough that you have an objective way to evaluate employee performance.

Once established and communicated, employees need feedback about their performance, not only during formal annual review times, but on an ongoing basis.

4. Provide Feedback

"How am I doing?"

It is no use having established objectives if employees do not know whether they are adequately meeting them. Since remote employees are away from the office and not part of the informal communication and feedback process that often takes place between managers and employees, it is important to establish formal channels and processes for providing feedback on performance.

Start from the premise that your employees want to do a good job. Their goal is to succeed. In order to do that, they need to receive regular and specific feedback from you about how they are doing. If you are remiss in letting them know when they have or have not met or exceeded your expectations, they cannot possibly improve their performance.

Establish a regular schedule for review and feedback. Evaluation should be directly tied to the job standards and goals that you have already established with the telecommuter. When creating your review schedule, ensure the following:

- Employees understand the process that will be used to review their performance. Explain how the review process will work, the criteria they will be measured on, and how frequently you will communicate with them about their performance.

- Feedback is provided regularly throughout the year — not just at the formal annual review.

- You are constructively candid. Be direct, but make sure that your constructive feedback is focused on objective job criteria, not personal characteristics or traits of the employee.

- Feedback is two-way. To maximize your relationship with your telecommuting staff, you will need feedback from them as well.

The time you're able to spend with your remote employee may be limited, so be sure to make the most of it. Reinforce positive behaviors and respond to unsatisfactory performance immediately.

Take advantage of all communication tools available to you to provide employees with timely and ongoing feedback.

5. Communication

Randstad US, a global staffing company, quickly mobilized 38,000 staff members to remote locations when COVID-19 hit. Recognizing the importance of managing these remote staff members effectively, the company immediately shared four tips to help managers make their remote workforce more efficient, says Jim Link, CHRO:

1. Schedule daily check-ins to keep employees engaged, align on goals, ensure accountability, and promote a sense of communication and collaboration.

2. Leverage free collaboration tools.

3. Focus on outcomes, not processes; studies have shown that when companies transition teams to remote work arrangements, productivity actually goes up by as much as 13%, so keep the focus on goals and outcomes.

4. Empower employees with the right technology.

Communication is of the utmost importance in any employee-manager relationship, but particularly with off-site staff. It is key to success. This cannot be stressed enough.

Putting efficient communication systems in place is your first major step as a manager of off-site staff, but it doesn't end there. The system must be easy to use, probably modified for certain individual employee needs, and continually updated and improved as problems or new strategies arise. Both employees and managers must be vigilant in their adherence to the systems of communication.

To be most effective at communicating with remote workers, find out the communication preferences of each of your staff members and be flexible in your interactions with them. Using only one system or schedule will not be an effective communication approach. Your goal is to develop interactions that work most effectively for all involved, and to ensure that all employees can meet their goals and be productive.

Ryan Prosser, CEO of Very, an Internet of Things design and development firm, transitioned more than 50 employees to be fully remote about two years ago. Since that time, he's discovered some communication best practices that have allowed him and his team to be productive and effective while working — and interacting — remotely. He recommends that other managers of remote staff do the following:

- **Choose a central platform to be your "nerve center" for communication:** Very uses Slack as the single source of sharing information and aiding in collaboration. The team created its own "ICYMI" (in case you missed it) bot so that people could up-vote important messages. Top messages are shared as a weekly digest on Mondays.

- **Integrate important HR information into your "nerve center":** Very moved all of its employee policies to Slack via an app integration so that all employees can pull up PTO and other policies instantly by asking a simple query, rather than needing to hunt for it through other platforms that they didn't use often, poring through emails, or asking HR.

- **Reassess how to define and measure accountability:** In the past, how effective people were in their job was perceived by how many hours they were in the office. As employers and teams now have no choice but to change how they evaluate productivity, this will spur many companies to reevaluate such KPIs (Key Performance Indicators) in the future. Companies will also rethink how different collaboration tools, which have been available for some time, can be used to maximum effect.

Working with a remote team and practicing effective communications, has allowed Prosser to tap into a wider talent pool and to focus on output and outcomes.

Michael Payne, founder of AnywhereWorks, points to communication as a critical component for any company, and especially for companies with dispersed employees, customers, clients, and other contacts. "Just as important to work communication is the freedom to connect in an informal setting, particularly in the current social isolation measures," he says, referring to COVID-19.

AnywhereWorks offers employees the opportunity to participate in "clubs" via the app, "people across the company can chat and share content on certain topics," he says. "I never realized how many aspiring bakers we had until I saw the Baking Club," he says. "I think we're all looking forward to meeting up again to try the cakes in person."

It's important to note, though, that communicating effectively doesn't necessarily mean communicating more. That's what Stefan Chekanov, CEO and cofounder of Brosix, an IM service, discovered after shifting staff off-site during COVID-19. Brosix, says Chekanov, has "always been a company that has valued a more flexible work setup, with several of our colleagues working remotely while the majority are office-based." It's in the company's DNA, he says; it specializes in providing teams with secure team communication solutions that are often used by remote teams.

"Even so," he says, "when the pandemic hit and offices began to shut down we were as hesitant and anxious as most companies were." Despite the fact that the company had experience with remote workers, they had never tried a fully remote setup. Some of their concerns included how team members would stay connected on a personal level and how they'd manage to hold effective meetings. They were pleasantly surprised on both counts, he says. "To our pleasant surprise, this time spent working remotely has been some of our most productive to date."

This has been, he says, partly due to the rallying effect that the crisis brought about, with everyone on the team eager to pitch in and help the team deal with this challenging situation and partly due to some of the inherent efficiencies that remote work brings to a team.

"Many of our colleagues reported being more focused while working from home, with less of the everyday distractions prevalent in an office space," he says. "In fact, we estimate that we've accomplished 15–20% more work while working remotely."

Staff also quickly adapted to entirely online meetings, and it led the entire team to really question the necessity of many meetings which, perhaps surprisingly has led to an overall reduction in meetings, Chekanov says.

6. Help Remote Teams Stay Connected

In a remote environment, says Payne, face-to-face contact is still important to keep projects on track. For face-to-face meetings his staff uses Teleport video. "You can invite as many people as you like to a secure digital meeting room, including people outside your company. The ShareScreen option has been invaluable in providing a solid foundation to abstract concepts and keeping everyone working from the same page — quite literally," he says.

Employees are also provided with access to their own employee HR portal, where they can request; view; and adjust holidays, sick days, and other breaks. "We use YoCoBoard for time tracking," Payne says. "Employees simply clock in at the start of their shift, clock out for extended periods away from their work and clock out at the end of the day to confirm their hours."

Staying connected can be particularly challenging when employees work in different time zones, especially when they're dispersed around the globe as is the case with Prime Plus Mortgages employees.

Loren Howard, company owner, has been able to instill a great deal of loyalty among his employees which definitely helps when it comes to keeping staff connected with him and with each other. The loyalty shows, he says, in that his overseas employees are willing to work largely US business hours, which coincide with Howard's hours. "When you work different hours than your employees, there are bound to be communication gaps," he said. "As a small company, it helps us a lot to all work the same hours."

To ensure high engagement with his employees who dot the globe, Howard said he created Prime Plus University, which involves a book club. They select a business-related book, which they all read; then review and discuss during weekly team meetings. "It's something fun. We can learn and grow as a team."

His team also has Skype chats "all of the time" to stay connected. In what he calls his "coaching" role, Howard said he believes it's his responsibility to share what he's learned through starting up, running, and owning businesses.

There's also his routine "positive focus," whereby they use a round-table format to share something positive related to their personal life, family, or work. "It's something I've always done, and as a leader, I like to share my personality with my team."

Howard says it can be a big challenge to manage remote teams, but "by taking the time to develop your team, you have an opportunity to hire the 'diamond in the rough.' I believe in building a close, genuine relationship that leads to employee development and loyalty."

FlexJobs, a fully virtual company, offers the following ideas on ways to help remote teams stay connected.

- **Coffee Chats:**

    Just because there's no break room to hang out in doesn't mean employees aren't taking breaks. In fact, as an employer, you should encourage your employees to take regular breaks to help improve their productivity. While you can't encourage them to meet at a coffee shop right now, you can schedule virtual coffee breaks with your team to stay connected while working from home.

    Let everyone know you'll be online at a certain time, taking your coffee break, and invite the team to join you. Or encourage others to set up their own virtual coffee breaks. Stay online, forget about work, and chat for a few minutes.

    And if you're looking for a conversation starter that doesn't involve, "How are you holding up?," try asking which coffee is better: the one at home or the one in the break room.

- **Ask a Question of the Week:**

    Since there's a good chance working from home will last for a while, post a random question in whatever chat application you use once a week. The questions can be short and sweet (What's your favorite season?), encourage longer answers (What's your favorite season and why?), be silly (Would you rather have a unicorn or a dinosaur as a pet?), or be somewhat serious (Which officemate would you prefer: dog or cat?).

    You'll probably get some interesting answers and learn a lot about your team in the process. The benefit here is that everybody doesn't have to be online at the same time for this to work. People can pop in and answer whenever it's convenient, and read through the responses when they need a quick and uplifting break.

- **Encourage Group Chats:**

  Your employees don't think about work all day every day. Many of them have outside interests and hobbies. In fact, some of your staff may get together and engage in these outside interests together!

  Even though everyone is working at home, that doesn't mean your staff wouldn't appreciate the chance to connect with coworkers with similar interests. So, set up some virtual groups to facilitate conversation.

  Create a group for people who like crafts or are into cooking so they can share recipes and projects. You can also create a parent group or even subgroups (single parents, parents of multiples) to share tips and advice. Or host virtual book clubs for the bookworms.

  These social groups let your remote staff bond and connect with people who have similar interests, but maybe don't work in the same department as they do, allowing them to learn more about each other and the company.

- **Virtual Lunches:**

  Like coffee breaks, lunch is another time when employees bond. Under normal circumstances, remote employees can meet coworkers for lunch in person (when they live nearby). Or they can go for lunch with family and friends.

  Of course, these are not normal circumstances. So, encourage staff to have a virtual lunch together. It's not quite like lunching with colleagues at a restaurant, but, for some, it's better than eating alone!

  You can also have a virtual office lunch. Set up a group conference and have the whole company get together and see what happens!

  For the truly adventurous, set up a "lunch roulette," once a week. Have people enter their name in a virtual "hat," and let the organizer randomly select who will meet up for a virtual lunch. It's a great way for coworkers on different teams to meet up and learn more about each other and their respective jobs.

- **Exchanges:**

  Meeting online is a great way to stay connected while working from home. However, sometimes there's nothing like getting a package or letter in the mail.

  Set up a cookie exchange so those who love to bake can send cookies to each other. For those who don't like to (or can't) cook, set up a pen-pal system so people can send cards and letters to each other.

- **Company Contests:**

  Just because you're not in an office doesn't mean you have to skip out on some "well-loved" traditions. Have the annual Ugly Sweater Contest or Halloween Costume Contest. For something a little less holiday-related, try a "craziest coffee mug" or "funniest pet moment" contest.

- **Company Challenges:**

  Company-wide challenges are a great way to get people together and encourage a little friendly competition. You can try a diet or exercise challenge, a journaling challenge, or even a LEGO building challenge. As long as it's something that gets people involved, entertained, and engaged in something fun for a few minutes, it's bound to be a hit.

- **Virtual Workouts:**

  Just because you can't get to the onsite company gym is no reason not to stay in shape. Consider organizing a group fitness break during the day. You can do yoga, chair stretching, or even a meditation session to keep everyone fit and healthy.

Working remotely shouldn't mean working alone and there are plenty of things that managers and supervisors can do to engage with workers and keep the lines of communication open. As FlexJobs says: "While team building is only one part of building a strong company culture, a few intentional and thoughtful gestures can go a long way toward making everyone feel like a part of the team, no matter where they are."

Not all of these techniques will work for all companies, and not just one will be enough in most cases to elicit the kind of engagement companies are looking for. Organizations need to think about their culture, their workforce, and their desired outcomes when determining what mix of communication channels and tools will work best for them. Ultimately the goal for any company should be motivating employees to help the company achieve its goals and objectives.

As Greg Hanover, CEO at Liveops, advises: "You have to be intentional about bringing the water cooler talk online, whether that be through Slack channels to show off your kids, pets, or ... for great work, monthly mixers and virtual happy hours, or small group conversations that allow you to take a break from work mode." Unless you set aside the time to do it, your staff will not have the opportunity to "meet" each other, he says. Engagement requires a "planned strategy with regularly delivered messages" to improve communication between all staff, whether on- or off-site.

7. Lessons from the Trenches

DJ Haddad is CEO of Haddad & Partners, a design shop. It's a creative and innovative company which lends itself to creative ideas for helping employees stay connected and engaged.

Haddad says: "I am lucky to work with the greatest team on the planet and somehow we have all become friends and created this amazing chemistry remotely over [Microsoft] Teams during this Pandemic." It may be hard to believe, but it's completely possible, he says.

The remote world of Haddad & Partners is "just like a real office environment," Haddad says. "We joke around, we make fun of each other, we make stupid GIFs of each other, we share high school prom photos, vacation photos, we live-chat while watching the Oscars, etc."

The company makes extensive use of Teams and has chats for everything. Haddad says a special summer program was created to offer unique virtual experiences every Friday at 3:00 p.m. as a way to end the week early and on a positive note. This series of virtual events is designed to #StretchSummer into September, he says. The events have previously included:

- Chalkroom Chat with former Chicago Bulls player, Scott Burrell. Early release after a Q&A session regarding Michael Jordan's wildly popular documentary *The Last Dance* in which Burrell was featured prominently.

- Feel the Burn Friday: Early release after virtual workouts led by the company's designer (who moonlights as a personal trainer), Christian Moy.

- Nama-stay, Nama-go: Early release after virtual yoga led by a Be Well Yoga Instructor.

- Walk into the Weekend a.k.a., Creative themed-walks: Early release after creative walk (staff search for certain colors or designs in nature and share on company Teams thread).

- Mindfulness Sessions: Early release after mindfulness session with meditation expert Gloria Schaffe.

- Freaky Friday: Early release after Chippendales virtual show at 3:00 p.m.

- Fridays Don't Have to be a Drag: Drag virtual show at 3:00 p.m.

"It feels like high school sometimes," Peace says, "but in the best possible way." The events and focus on fun are an effort to acknowledge the tough times everyone is operating in and the ongoing stress related not only to remote work but to employees who are parents and stressing out over getting their kids back to school — or whether they will be able to go back to school.

These simple activities don't have to cost a lot but can go a long way toward establishing team cohesiveness, minimizing stress, and generating loyalty and engagement among employees.

Chapter 10

MOTIVATE OFF-SITE STAFF

Shubhabrata Mohanty is CIO at Altimetrik, a computer software firm that works with Fortune 100 companies to achieve digital transformation. Although the company already had some employees working from home before the impacts of COVID-19 were felt, there were still adjustments that needed to be made.

In the US, says Mohanty, "work-from-home was an easier transition as some of our employees were already 100% remote and others were in the office part of the week." In India, though, he says, most employees worked in the office. "Moving to 100% work-from-home was a bigger change for many." The company, though, moved quickly to accommodate employees during the adjustment, he says.

"We provided devices to our employees to use to connect to a global online network from home so they were able to interact with coworkers and customers in different regions. This helped us to quickly adopt the work-from-home model with few challenges." However, he adds, "It may be more challenging to adapt to work-from-home policies for newly onboarded employees, but technology has greatly supported this shift."

Altimetrik has offices and employees in a number of regions in the US, India, Singapore, Uruguay, UAE, and Japan.

"Although each of our regions had different readiness levels to the coronavirus pandemic, all of them converted to 100% work-from-home quickly," Mohanty says. In some regions, this was a completely new way of operating and collaborating with others. In these cases, MS Teams and Zoom allow for team members to stay connected and continue to work with one another. Having video connection and seeing coworkers may not be the same as in-person interaction, but it does close the gap in feeling remote. The transition was very quick and now employees seamlessly work and collaborate remotely without losing momentum or productivity.

The key difference between work-from-home and work-from-office is in-person interaction, says Mohanty. Without in-person interaction, collaboration in the workplace has become virtual, he says, predicting that a virtual mode of interaction will make the traditional top-down management structure that generally prevails in the workplace no longer relevant. Teams, he says, "will be more spread out virtually and globally and it will slowly evolve into a flat management structure."

In addition, Mohanty notes, in a work-from-home structure "management style is shifting toward outcome-driven rather than task-driven and employees are feeling more empowered than before. Their focus is completely on delivering results instead of spending extended hours at work.

"However, some employees may feel that they are spending more time on meetings just to show their presence. So, building a trust-based culture in remote collaboration is key in making the work-from-home model successful."

It's important for companies and their leaders to recognize the isolation that can develop in a setting where team members are dispersed and not physically connected.

"While work-from-home has given more flexibility to employees, at the same time it may not be a comfortable situation for many to work in isolation for extended periods of time. Employees who thrive with in-person interaction and enjoy their presence at the office are definitely impacted by this and are having difficulties maintaining their morale and productivity," Mohanty says.

To address this, he says, Altimetrik has "institutionalized multiple models of engaging employees with remote activities during breaks like group dance, music, sharing their WFH experiences, letting their kids interact with others, and discussing their interests outside of work."

Managers have also created ways to come together. "We have started remote ideation programs where leaders share their ideas for new business solutions or share their experiences with customer pain points," Mohanty says. "This has given a platform for leaders to think beyond what they do on a daily basis. We are running programs like Think-Thursdays, a tech-talk series, and Ideathon, an innovation challenge program where employees share their learning with others and bring new ideas to the table. It is a new world which requires a new model and a new way of thinking about communication and collaboration. We are ensuring every contribution from our employees is recognized and we are leveraging our digital wall and rewards platform for instant recognition and appreciation. Our focus is shifted to a quadrilateral model of work, learn, innovate, and have fun."

At Lucidworks, a San Francisco-based search AI tech leader, chief people officer Ellen Petry Leanse says that the company has launched a number of measures to help create solidarity for its global workforce. These include virtual roundtables on Zoom to review company benefits, including telemedicine and mental health support, and hangouts to connect employees over video in a water-cooler-type setting (including "opposite hours" hangouts for team members who work in locations with time differences of 12+ hours).

While the company has provided staff with Zoom background screens branded with their company color and logo to help video calls "look more professional," Petry Lense says that she "loved seeing my teammate Bill virtualize a swirling Aurora Borealis as his background in my team's weekly all-hands." Humor, she says, helps boost the immune system so: "We welcome any opportunity to laugh and let the stress levels dissipate." It's great, she says, that this is possible "even across the airwaves."

The ability to make these connections on an ongoing basis can go a long way toward helping remote staff feel engaged and connected.

One of the greatest fears that remote staff have is that they will become invisible. They worry about being out of touch and overlooked for key assignments and promotions. As a manager, you should be aware of this concern and take steps to ensure that your remote workers maintain their involvement and visibility within the organization. There are a number of ways in which you can do this:

- Be honest about the changes that will occur when an employee is working off-site. Obviously, relationships will change. Address the issue head on and help the employee work through his or her concerns.

- Emphasize to the remote employee the role that he or she plays in maintaining visibility. Encourage off-site staff to take advantage of all communication tools available to them and stress the importance of establishing frequent and effective communication links to the head office.

- Provide support staff and other staff members with the home phone numbers and email addresses of off-site staff members so they won't be left out of general office communications.

- Keep in touch with off-site staff and provide frequent updates about what's happening back at the head office. Consider email newsletters that can provide regular reports on news and events.

- Don't overlook off-site employees when selecting members for team projects, tasks, or promotions.

- Schedule regular and frequent trips to the office so off-site employees have the opportunity to interact with other members of the staff.

- Include team-building activities at regular meetings.

- Schedule frequent evaluation sessions.

- Be flexible and willing to change your style of communication or consider unique modes of interaction based on the needs of individual employees.

- Make sure that off-site staff are offered the same professional growth opportunities as the rest of the staff. Some ways of doing this might include:

  - Allowing off-site staff to join professional organizations related to their current jobs or jobs they are interested in.

- Sending off-site staff to courses to enhance their skills or help them develop additional skills.

- Working with off-site staff on career advancement within the organization.

- Recommending off-site staff for task forces and committees.

Jordan Peace, CEO of Fringe, a lifestyle benefits startup, notes that while many companies are known for exceptional onsite perks "such as gym memberships, ping pong tables, and office snacks" employees now working in a world of WFH are missing out on those perks. "COVID-19 has created an urgency for employers to critically reassess their benefits offerings to ensure that they're meeting the needs of employees today," says Peace. He suggests that employers look for solutions that prioritize immediate, rather than long-term needs, that offer simplicity of use and recognize the diversity of employees' lifestyles.

"One way to achieve this is to offer a personalized benefits marketplace, where employees are free to choose the benefits they want, whether that's a subscription to Netflix, or an on-demand fitness offering like Dance Body," Peace says. "This ensures benefits are serving a real need, and bringing an immediate and meaningful impact on the day-to-day."

Employers should consider how some of their onsite perks might be able to be modified and brought to employees working from home. "For example, replacing a membership to a specific gym, with a subscription to virtual workout classes," Peace suggests. "By offering an array of different apps and services, employees are able to select those that make the biggest difference in their lives. For example, working parents would likely appreciate access to a monthly activity box for kids to keep them engaged and entertained while at home. Meanwhile, a single, young professional who doesn't like to cook, would appreciate access to a food delivery service." What's most important, Peace says, is meeting employees' individual needs.

1. Managing Both Onsite and Off-site Staff

There will, of course, be situations where managers are responsible for managing staff who are both onsite and off-site. That can require some special finessing to ensure that all needs are met and that communication channels are fluid and open. Especially, during COVID-19, as some employees were required to work onsite and others able to work remotely, resentment is an issue. That's was true, though, before COVID-19 emerged and will continue to be true after the risk has subsided. As we've seen, despite great advances in technology, there are still some jobs that simply can't be performed remotely. Chances are, therefore, that managers will be called upon to manage employees in both settings.

Telework has long been perceived as a potential benefit for employees, allowing flexibility and saving them time and money that would have been spent on commuting, business attire, and other expenses. In 2020, telework gained another associated benefit: personal safety.

"During uncertain times and periods of change within organizations, authentic and transparent communications play a critical role," said Kate Bullinger, New York City-based president of United Minds, a management consultancy specializing in organizational transformation. A "consistent cadence of communications is key," she said, "to help manage employee anxieties and increase employee trust."

That continues to be true, however, even without the fear of a pandemic.

Matt Erhard is managing partner with Summit Search Group, a recruitment and executive search firm based in Winnipeg, Manitoba. One major complaint from remote workers, Erhard said, is feeling isolated or left out of the loop. "Managers can help prevent this by giving remote staff easy, clear channels to communicate with both coworkers and managers throughout their workday," he advises.

Daily email check-ins and memos aren't enough, he said. "Simulating an office environment with an open chat space or virtual water-cooler program can be a great way to help workers at home feel like part of the team."

2. Additional Tips for Managers of Off-site Staff

The remote employee/manager relationship is an evolving one. It will be continually fine-tuned to suit the changing needs of the business, the individual needs of each employee, and the professional growth of the manager. Always seek advice and examples from other managers and also from remote staff members, whether they are working for you or not.

Remember that a trusting relationship is critical. Try not to over-manage your off-site staff members, making them feel as though they are under constant surveillance. Be careful, though, to find the balance between over-managing and ignoring off-site staff. Try not to become too much of an absentee manager. Maintaining the right amount of contact with your off-site employees will allow them to feel involved without feeling stifled.

You are bound to face some challenges in your alternative work relationships, particularly if these arrangements are new to you and/or your organization. Good organization and communication skills are your best combative measures. Help your off-site staff members organize their work. Don't expect perfection, and don't expect everyone to be successful. Some employees adjust more readily to a remote working relationship than others. Working remotely may not work for everyone. When it doesn't, take immediate steps to develop a more workable solution.

Companies have found ways to address the common pitfalls of managing remote workers. American Express, for example, assigns off-site staff a "buddy" in the home office to be sure they are informed. Off-site employees are encouraged to spend time during work hours talking with their buddies about work-related issues to keep abreast of office developments and boost morale. Communication, of course, is key and can't be emphasized enough. Having a point person in the office that is not the employee's manager can help ensure that interactions are taking place regularly and that remote employees feel included.

The strategies and techniques necessary to motivate off-site staff are the same as those you should already be using with your on-site employees. The following are some strategies that will work with employees both onsite and off-site:

- **Listen to your off-site staff members' concerns:** Make sure that you are sincere in listening to your employees and that you give fair and honest consideration to their questions and concerns.

- **Be available:** Make sure that your off-site employees have ready access to you by phone, email, or in person.

- **Share information:** Off-site employees have a heightened need to feel included. When you share information with them, they will feel more involved in what's happening at the company. This can be as simple as letting them know about an employee's going-away party or as involved as reviewing information about the organization's strategic plan.

- **Give ample recognition for a job well done:** Provide off-site staff with frequent feedback about how they're doing and make sure that you share their accomplishments and achievements with onsite staff.

- **Provide opportunities for professional growth:** As previously discussed, remote employees, like any employees, need to be motivated by opportunity for growth.

- **Treat all employees as individuals:** It is rare to find two individuals who have the same skills or personal objectives. While one off-site employee may react favorably to infrequent contact and open-ended expectations, another may require frequent visits to the office and very clear and specific direction. Take the time to get to know your off-site staff members and to understand their individual goals and objectives.

- **Be open to new ideas:** Employee feedback is important to any company's success. Listen carefully to every idea presented and give each fair consideration. If you decide to use an idea, make sure that you give credit to the individual who made the suggestion.

- **Have fun!:** All work and no play can make all of us dull. When employees have been working nonstop for a period of time, they need and appreciate a little time off. Allow some breaks and take time to celebrate successes.

There are many ways to show your appreciation to employees. Be creative.

3. Lessons from the Trenches

Andrew Meadows is senior vice president at Ubiquity Retirement + Savings, in San Francisco, a company that employs 85 people — 85% of them working from home. Formed in 1999, the company is one of the first online 401k companies to provide retirement plans to small businesses, offering a low-cost option to small businesses and individuals. As the company celebrated its 20th year, the original business plan of founder and CEO Chad Parks recognized that employees do their best work when they can take care of things on the home front — a work/life balance would be essential to his business model.

In 2010 and 2011, Ubiquity had a partnership with Intuit 401k, which required opening a sales office in Austin, Texas. "It was our first office outside of San Francisco," Meadows says. "As the partnership wrapped up, we knew we had some very valuable employees that we wanted to keep. That's when we started creating more and more opportunities for remote employees."

Today, 85% of the company's employees are based at home. To ensure engagement, employees meet with their leaders, virtually, once a week. Team meetings are weekly or every other week. Each Tuesday, the company holds a popular ten-minute meeting called Vital Factors to share key business metrics along with promotions, birthdays, etc. "It's an opportunity for each employee to turn their camera on and connect to celebrate successes," Meadows says. "At least 85% of employees attend weekly."

Company technology also provides a virtual breakroom, which mimics spontaneous water-cooler activity. There are quarterly company meetings and Red Rovers, in which employees have opportunities to solve problems for the business. A huge and popular event, at least prior to the pandemic, Meadows says, is Reimagine, which is tied to the company's anniversary each August. Every employee flies to San Francisco, where the company rents a space large enough for all employees to work side by side for a week. "It's a way to validate that it's easy to stay connected and be team partners, even though we're working remotely," Meadows explains. "We spend time 'hacking' the business to look for ways to improve it."

Meadows says surveys show proof of engagement from employees working remotely. In the past two years, the net promoter score has doubled. "It shows that the culture and success belong to everybody."

Community involvement is high as well, he says. In addition to knowing that the company funds a variety of causes through its Ubiquity Gives programs, employees are funding causes that aren't so local. With three days per year of volunteer time off, employees clean up after hurricanes and wildfires that have affected their home areas. Alternatively, they can use the time to chaperone a child's school field trip, to keep work/home life in balance. "We ask that employees take photos of their activities and post them to share with colleagues," Meadows says.

All of these efforts are designed to ensure that remote workers are engaged and involved with their managers, each other, and their customers. It's a model that has worked for Ubiquity and one that Meadows thinks can, and will, work for many other companies long after COVID-19 has passed and employers can — but may choose not to — bring employees back to the workplace.

Chapter 11

MEASURING OUTCOMES

Properly implemented and conscientiously managed, your alternative work arrangements should prove highly beneficial to both your company and your employees. When the operation is running smoothly, workers should be more productive, overhead costs should be reduced, and employee retention should show improvement. The overall success (or failure) of the program should be as rigorously monitored as the fine details of its operations.

Patricia Elias, chief legal and people officer with ServiceSource, says the company has been pleasantly surprised by the productivity their staff has sustained, even boosted, during COVID-19. "Working from home in a pandemic, with schools closed and spouses, partners, and roommates all at home, is much different than a typical work-from-home environment," she says. Still she says, "Across the board our productivity has improved since we moved to a work-from-home model." As a sales and customer success company, she says, "Our productivity is relatively easier to measure — if we drive more business for our clients, we see success." In addition, she notes, staff engagement is also on the rise. "Our most recent pulse-engagement survey saw increases in most of our global locations. We think our quick reaction to the pandemic, priority of keeping employees safe, and demonstrating our core value of caring helped in this regard."

One of the biggest mental challenges for many managers is to shift their focus to actual outcomes rather than time on the clock. This runs contrary to how many managers have viewed employee management for the bulk of their careers. But historically, managers tend to miss the true measure of productivity.

"Focus on results, not 8 to 5. Who cares if your employee takes a nap in the middle of the day and then is energized to power through later in the afternoon?" says Tara Bethell of Copper Quail Consulting. "Who cares if an employee writes at 10 o'clock in the evening or 4 o'clock in the morning if that's when their creativity strikes? Who cares if an employee stops working in the middle of the day to snuggle with their kids or pets who will not be with us forever? I don't care about these things," Bethell says. "What I do care about are results. Are my employees delivering on their projects on time and with great quality? Are they responsive to clients and coworkers? If the answers are yes, it doesn't matter how they structure their day at home."

Marlo Green, SPHR, SHRM, owner of Green Ocean HR, agrees and says he has actually seen an increase in employee productivity with the shift to remote work. "I passionately believe that for the most part, productivity as a whole has increased, allowing employees to work from home," he says.

"It is important for managers to understand that it is not realistic for employees to sit at a desk from 8 to 5 and only get up for lunch or a quick bathroom break," Green adds. "For my employees, I give them the opportunity to check out as needed to balance home and life."

There are times, says Green, when employees start work early before the kids wake and check out for a couple of hours and then come back online. When you can't monitor time, you can and should monitor output.

To ensure the job is getting done and everyone is on the same page, Green created an MS Planner page to show everyone the top three to five goals the company needs to accomplish during work from home. This, says Green, allowed his team to update their information while keeping him in the loop on a regular basis.

One form of assessment or monitoring that some management experts feel may do more harm than good is remote monitoring. While technology exists to monitor employees to ensure that they're "really working," using this type of technology can erode trust.

Laura Handrick, contributing HR professional at Choosing Therapy and owner of an HR and business consulting agency, says: "Personally I don't believe in the kind of draconian surveillance that includes monitoring employees on video using computer-screen cameras," she says. "Instead, I recommend setting clear, defined performance metrics that give the employee flexibility in when and how they get their work done remotely." For instance, in a call center environment, she says this may translate to a number of documented calls required each day or week; in a sales environment, it may look like a monthly or weekly sales volume or revenue target; in a content shop, it may be the number of social media posts, or completed articles.

"By using work targets, key performance indicators, or measurable productivity metrics, the organization is much more likely to reach its objectives," Handrick says. "Goal-oriented work gives employees a sense of control and prevents them from feeling undermined by add-on supervision software, or having their boss spy on their PC to see if they're really working."

For remote work arrangements to succeed, there must be a level of trust between remote workers and their managers and the organization. At the same time, it's understandable that managers want to have a way to monitor staff and their productivity.

After all, that's a key part of managers' jobs. With the need to continue remote work for the foreseeable future, this is a critical time to begin thinking about how you can monitor and measure employee contributions based on output (specific goals and objectives) rather than input (time).

1. Finding the Right Balance

Mark Webster is cofounder of Authority Hacker, an online marketing education company. The business has been fully remote for more than six years, "so we're well acquainted with the pros and cons of running a work-from-home operation," says Webster. One of the main barriers, he says, is the inability for companies — especially very large companies — to monitor team performance to really understand whether staff can work productively from home without sacrificing quality output.

"We know that this is possible — there's no doubt about that. However, for a goal-driven, corporate office, things are inevitably different than a small ten-person business like ours," he says.

While some companies see screen tracking and recording as a "go-to" method for productivity monitoring, Webster believes that this type of monitoring is inherently flawed. "It doesn't paint a full picture and one can easily appear to be active in one of these tools, yet not be hitting any of their goals. Not only that, but it can be incredibly harmful to employee productivity if they feel bound to their computer eight hours a day without break to please the software they're using."

Finding the right balance between tracking goals and ensuring employees are remaining productive is crucial to properly executing remote work, Webster says. "Come down too hard for the wrong reasons and you'll end up with a demotivated team that probably won't really understand what they've been doing wrong. Become too lax with goals and productivity tracking and liberties may be taken; that's not to say people that do this are bad people, it's just human nature," he says.

At iGMS, a SaaS company specializing in developing short-term rental management software, CMO Inna Shevchenko says that Hubstaff is used to monitor and measure team productivity. "The app helps us analyze each member's activity and their weekly performance," she says. "It allows us not only to monitor productivity but also to make optimizations to improve efficiency if needed. By doing so, we're able to figure out where the major bottlenecks are and take action accordingly. In addition, collecting such data enable our top management to be in sync with the teams at all times thanks to the powerful reporting features of the app."

Doing the tracking, says Shevchenko, helps the company use time wisely and effectively. The app, she says, also helps employees maintain a healthy work-life balance and stay motivated for future project achievements. In addition to monitoring the data available through Hubstaff, Shevchenko holds weekly one-on-ones with each team member to ensure KPIs are on track and that employees have what they need to complete their tasks. It's an approach that has worked well for their team, she says.

Max Harland is CEO of Dentaly, a free source of independent information on dental care and oral health problems. Monitoring staff productivity and output doesn't have to be complex, Harland points out. "A simple way to measure the productivity of remote employees is to have them keep track of all the work they do and when they do it," he says. This can be as simple as tracking tasks completed in a Word or Excel document. "It's best for them to keep track of their work on a daily basis," he says. "At the end of each week, have them send you a recap email with the log of all they were able to accomplish on the days they worked," he suggests. Doing so can also be beneficial for employee growth, Harland says. Tracking activity can provide both an ongoing record of accomplishments and comparative information to help monitor productivity over time.

It Works Media created its own project planner to help oversee employee activity when the company was forced to lock down during COVID-19, says Steve Pritchard, managing director. It's just a simple spreadsheet maintained on the company's shared drive that allows everyone to feed into. "It requires all personnel to log which tasks they've completed and how long they have spent on them, on a daily basis," he says. It's a kind of tracking that allows transparency in terms of how long it takes for projects to be completed. "We can observe if their responsibilities are taking more or less time than usual, along with assigning accountability to every task. Then we can assess the quality of each piece of work as normal to ensure that standards aren't slipping."

It's been a highly effective system for It Works Media, Pritchard says. "It's quick and effortless for staff to update, taking around 3.5% of their working day." That, he says, "lets them get on with their roles without us having to micromanage their every move as they can record their output before finishing up for the day." And, he says, "it means there is nowhere to hide for those who slack off, as we'd be able to see if they're undertaking less than they would in the office."

Clearly, it's important to establish methods of evaluating the effectiveness of any alternative work arrangements as well as the morale of both off- and on-site staff. This can be done by measuring output, by surveying those involved in the program, and through direct observation. Technology also affords the means to evaluate program outcomes by measuring how many employees use remote access, for instance; or by keeping track of how long online sessions last, when employees are logging in, and how frequently they connect.

The process of evaluating performance should be built in from the outset. Both qualitative and quantitative information can be used for assessment. The criteria you select for assessment should be based on the objectives you initially established. For example, if your primary objective for allowing for flexible work arrangements was to improve employee morale and reduce turnover, you might include a qualitative measurement of morale, perhaps self-reports from off-site employees and other staff members, as well as quantitative measures of turnover. If your primary objective was to reduce office space costs, again, you should be able to apply quantitative measures of costs based on a before-and-after comparison.

Depending on your objectives and the measures of success you've selected, there are a variety of sources from which to obtain information. These sources may include individuals, for instance, off-site staff members, their managers, onsite employees, and customers. Sources may also include data, such as turnover data, office-supply expense data, and productivity records.

Feedback to the participants in the program is very important. Share the results of whatever you're measuring and involve off-site staff (and their onsite colleagues) in any discussions on how to improve results.

2. Why Alternative Work Arrangements Fail

As we have seen in this book, there are a number of reasons why these relationships may fail; but we have also seen that with appropriate methods of program implementation and management, there are many more reasons why such relationships should succeed.

Creating successful work relationships with off-site staff requires careful attention to detail, flexibility in responding to unique personal and departmental needs, clear objectives, and identified methods of monitoring and measuring the success of alternative work arrangements. The specifics of each situation will vary by company and by position, but these general needs remain consistent across all programs.

Not every alternative work relationship will be a successful one. Sometimes off-site employees decide that they miss the interaction and security of the traditional office setting. Or you may decide that productivity or service to customers is suffering from the alternative work arrangement. In either case, it is important to act quickly to remedy the situation.

Unresolved issues can have a negative impact in a number of ways. There may be direct monetary costs to the organization. There may be productivity costs. There will almost certainly be morale problems, especially if you fail to take action. Other employees will quickly become frustrated if remote workers are not pulling their weight.

A common mistake made by managers is to wait to see if the issue will resolve itself. Few people welcome conflict, and — at least initially — it appears far easier to avoid conflict than to confront it. In fact, avoiding a problem may actually result in greater frustration, effort, and cost to the organization at a later date.

If a problem surfaces, address it immediately. Just as when addressing performance issues with onsite employees, your feedback should be immediate, predictable, impersonal, and consistent. Approach the employee as soon as the issue has been noticed or reported. Selecting the appropriate tool to communicate with the employee is very important. While a minor issue (a reminder to turn in a report, for example) may be handled via email, other more critical issues (e.g., a customer complaint about lack of availability) may require a face-to-face meeting. Make sure that you don't use technology as a means of avoiding uncomfortable situations.

Your comments should remain focused on the task and the objective measures of performance you have established, not on the personal habits or characteristics of the employee. Do not criticize a remote worker for something that an employee in a comparable position at the workplace would not be criticized for. The agreement you created at the beginning of the relationship can provide a good frame of reference and guide for addressing problems in the relationship.

Finally, don't treat the employee as an adversary. Address the issue without lecturing, nagging, or losing your temper. Make sure to allow the employee an opportunity to tell his or her side of the story, and be sure to listen with an open mind.

If a problem arises, you will have to discuss the situation with the off-site employee. During this discussion, you should —

- have notes and make use of them,
- explain the facts as completely as possible,
- ask the employee for his or her perspective,
- expect and allow some emotional venting,
- be specific about the consequences of continued problems, and
- provide a system for follow-up.

If the situation progresses or becomes worse, it may be necessary to either terminate the alternative work arrangement or terminate the employment relationship.

In either case, it is important that you have documented the issues that have led to your decision and that you address the problem immediately and objectively.

When a performance-related incident occurs, record the date it happened, what specifically occurred, and the interaction you had with the employee. Inform the employee of each infraction and ensure that they understand implications if future occurrences take place.

Your goal in dealing with performance issues is not to move quickly to terminate the work arrangement or employment relationship, but to maintain a productive and effective employee. In providing the employee with information about behaviors or actions that are inconsistent with policy or expectations, you should also provide coaching and assistance in improving employee behavior. Perhaps more training is required. Perhaps the tools available to the employee are insufficient to perform the job effectively. However, do not hesitate to terminate the work arrangement if it is not meeting the needs of the department or the organization.

3. Lessons from the Trenches

John J. Thompson, Esq., is a partner with Thompson & Skrabaek, PLLC, in New York City; he focuses his practice on employment law, commercial litigation, and early stage startups.

As courts began to reopen in June 2020, Thompson expects to see more clients asking for help related to work-from-home policies, advice, and best practices.

One issue he sees that working from home will impact is "time on the clock." While he says there are "great software systems that bigger companies use for their teams to clock in and clock out with the computer," he adds that there are still issues, for example, when a supervisor calls after hours and asks for a document or that a project be completed.

"Generally, hourly workers need to be paid and paid overtime for any activities — on or off the clock."

As the pandemic continues, more companies will be seeking help from attorneys, Thompson predicts.

"In the pre-COVID days, employees might be allowed to work occasionally from home. It was pretty vague. Now, we need structure in terms of data security, productivity, and other concerns."

And, he says, there will be even more questions if employees are using personal computer equipment. What happens when documents need to be gathered during discovery lawsuits? Personal materials could be mixed in with the company's commercial business documents.

What, he asks, happens if a home-based employee complains about a hostile work environment stemming from a supervisor? Witnesses are essential in such complaints, but how will that be handled when so much of the communication would be one to one in a home-based environment. It will be hard to challenge or disprove what the supervisor said or did in such cases.

Thompson said it will take a while to see the effects COVID will have on remote workforces.

"Perhaps in 6 to 12 months we will see issues become more visible," he says.

Thompson's advice to employers as they seek to manage more work-from-home opportunities:

- Sit down and think about activities and productivity and how the workplace has changed. Employers need to predict issues.

- Review data security and timekeeping issues. There needs to be more clarity around working after hours, checking email after hours, and other obligations to protect from overtime lawsuits.

- Consider all compliance and legal risks and how they would be handled.

- Think more specifically about communication. In addition to check-ins from the supervisor, should departments such as HR take a more active role in reaching out to remote teams and individuals?

- Consider employee privacy and ensure they are accountable for work. There needs to be a structure in which it's easy to oversee employees who work from home. You want productivity without the boss looking over your shoulder.

- Review and implement technology options that allow access to files and ability to track what employees are doing. Should those systems be running at all times? This can raise thorny issues, he said. "What if you wanted to write a private email to HR about your boss, but you feared that your boss would be watching you write the email."

- Create work-from-home policies and add them to the Employee Handbook. Some companies will want to create specific policies and ask that employees sign a document to acknowledge that they have read and understand the work-from-home policies. Although the Employee Handbook is considered part of a contract between employee and employer, many companies also create the document for signing. "Some policies may have been rendered absurd because work and home life have been commingled," Thompson says.

- Companies that deal with highly sensitive documents, banking, for example, may want to provide laptops for their employees who work from home. There is greater liability for these companies. And, it can be an issue of fairness to employees who have children and other working adults in the household. One family computer will not be sufficient.

DOWNLOAD KIT

Please enter the URL you see in the box below into your computer web browser to access and download the kit.

> www.self-counsel.com/updates/remotemgnt/20kit.htm

The download kit includes:

- Sample telecommuting policy
- Checklist to help you manage remotely
- Sources and further reading

OTHER TITLES OF INTEREST FROM SELF-COUNSEL PRESS

Avoid Small-Business Hell

Jack Borden
ISBN: 978-1-77040-251-5
$14.95 USD/$16.95 CAD

Find success as a small-business entrepreneur! For every attempt to create a successful small business, there are dozens of trip wires and trap doors that send you to Small Business Hell. Jack Borden, creator of the Faster, Cheaper, Better program of entrepreneurial excellence, guides you through the challenges and helps you start and operate a small firm that becomes profitable and sustainable.

This book discusses the many challenges and pitfalls entrepreneurs may face in business. It includes stories from many different small-business entrepreneurs so readers can learn from their mistakes. It also includes an exclusive downloadable forms kit with business forms to help readers stay organized and keep their businesses on the path to success.

The GiveBack Economy
Social Responsibility Practices for Business and Nonprofit

Peter Miller and Carla Langhorst
ISBN: 978-1-77040-294-2
$17.95 USD/$19.95 CAD

Do well by doing good! Social enterprise and social entrepreneurship is a field that is heating up. It is a business idea that has been fringe for a number of years, but that is growing more mainstream. Increasingly, the idea of social responsibility will be part of every business person's agenda, especially as younger generations become of age and take on ownership and participation in business.

Authors Carla Langhorst and Peter Miller brought their varied business and teaching experiences together to write *The GiveBack Economy*, a book to help readers navigate this new world built on change and doing social good. The book also includes an exclusive downloadable forms kit of useful forms and resources.

The Business Transition Coach
Your guide to succession planning, exit strategies, and preparing for the big handoff

Wayne Vanwyck
ISBN: 978-1-77040-329-1
$19.95 USD - $26.95 CAD

Millions of business owners intend to move on from their businesses in the next several years yet only a small percentage of them have a written succession plan. Those who don't plan their business transition ahead of time may have to kiss all their creativity, passion, and hard work goodbye as they face a market soon to be glutted with businesses for sale.

The Business Transition Coach: Your guide to succession planning, exit strategies, and preparing for the big handoff is your guide to transitioning out of any business. Author Wayne Vanwyck shows you through experience and case studies how planning this transition can increase the value of your business, increase its profitability, and keep your options open.

Let this book be your helpful companion on the road to transitioning out of your business and into the next phase of your life.